BRAM STOKER'S
DRACULA
THE CRITICAL FEAST

*An Annotated Reference of
Early Reviews & Reactions, 1897-1913*

BRAM STOKER'S
DRACULA
THE CRITICAL FEAST

*An Annotated Reference of
Early Reviews & Reactions, 1897-1913*

*Compiled and Annotated, with an Introduction,
by* John Edgar Browning

*Bibliographical Afterword
by* J. Gordon Melton

the apocryphile press
BERKELEY, CA
www.apocryphile.org

Apocryphile Press
1700 Shattuck Ave #81
Berkeley, CA 94709
www.apocryphile.org

Copyright © 2011 by John Edgar Browning
"Bibliographical Afterword" Copyright © 2011 by J. Gordon Melton

Printed in the United States of America
ISBN 978-1-937002-21-3

All rights reserved. No part of the front or back matter may be used or reproduced in any manner whatsoever without written permission except in the case of brief quotations embodied in critical articles or reviews.

Frontispiece: Abraham (Bram) Stoker, ca. 1906

Title Page: Illustration of "Mr. Bram Stoker" from The Bookman 14, no. 79 (April 1898): 21. (Image published with permission of ProQuest. Further reproduction is prohibited without permission.)

CONTENTS

Dedication... 10
Acknowledgments... 11
A Note on the Selections and Editorial Procedure..................... 12

Introduction: The Myth of *Dracula*'s Critical Reception..........13
John Edgar Browning

Reviews & Reactions
  1. *The Daily News* [London] (May 27, 1897).....................22
  2. *Lloyd's Weekly Newspaper* [London] (May 30, 1897)...26
  3. *The Daily Mail* [London] (June 1, 1897).......................28
  4. *Pall Mall Gazette* [London] (June 1, 1897)...................29
  5. *The Booksellers' Review* [London] (June 3, 1897)........31
  6. *The Daily Telegraph* [London] (June 3, 1897)..............32
  7. *The Bristol Times and Mirror* (June 5, 1897)................36
  8. *The Glasgow Herald* (June 10, 1897)............................39
  9. *The Speaker* [London] (June 12, 1897).........................40
  10. *The Academy: A Weekly Review of Literature, Science, and Art (Fiction Supplement)* [London] (June 12, 1897)...41
  11. *Illustrated London News* (June 12 [or July 17], 1897) 43
  12. *The Manchester Guardian* (June 15, 1897) 44
  13. *Westminster Gazette* [London] (June 15, 1897)...........45
  14. *The Stage* [London] (June 17, 1897)..............................46

15. *The Liverpool Daily Post* (June 17, 1897) 48
16. *Country Life Illustrated* [London] (June 19, 1897) 52
17. *The Athenaeum* [London] (June 26, 1897) 55
18. *Punch, or The London Charivari* (June 26, 1897) 56
19. *Vanity Fair: A Weekly Show of Political, Social and Literary Wares* [London] (June 29, 1897) 57
20. *St. James' Gazette* [London] (June 30, 1897) 58
21. *Belgravia: A London Magazine* (July 1897) 60
22. *The British Weekly* [London] (July 1, 1897) 60
23. *Saturday Review of Politics, Literature, Science and Art* [London] (July 3, 1897) 65
24. *National Observer, and British Review of Politics, Economics, Literature, Science, and Art* [London] (July 3, 1897) 66
25. *Black and White: A Weekly Illustrated Record and Review* [London] (July 10, 1897) 67
26. *The Spectator: A Weekly Review of Politics, Literature, Theology, and Art* [London] (July 31, 1897) 68
27. *The Academy: A Weekly Review of Literature, Science, and Art* [London] (July 31, 1897) 69
28. *The Bookman: An Illustrated Literary Journal* [New York] (August 1897) 70
29. *The Observer* [London] (August 1, 1897) 71
30. *Daily Mail* [London] (August 6, 1897) 72
31. *Publishers' Circular and Booksellers' Record of British and Foreign Literature* [London] (August 7, 1897) 72
32. *The Guardian* [Manchester] (August 11, 1897) 73
33. Letter from Arthur Conan Doyle to Bram Stoker (August 20, 1897) 75
34. *The Times* [London] (August 23, 1897) 76
35. *The New York Dramatic Mirror* (August 21, 1897) 78

36. *The Bookseller: A Newspaper of British and Foreign Literature* (September 3, 1897) 78
37. *The Liverpool Mercury* (September 15, 1897) 79
38. *London Quarterly Review* (October 1897) 80
39. *The South Australian Register* [Adelaide, South Australia] (November 6, 1897) 81
40. *The Argus* [Melbourne, Victoria, Australia] (November 6, 1897) 82
41. *The Speaker: A Review of Politics, Letters, Science, and the Arts* [London] (January 1, 1898) 86
42. *The Advertiser* [Adelaide, South Australia] (January 22, 1898) 88
43. *The Literary World* [London] (February 28, 1898) 88
44. *The Hawkes Bay Herald* [Napier, New Zealand] (April 23, 1898) 89
45. *The Land of Sunshine* [Los Angeles] (June 1899) 92
46. *The Publishers' Weekly* [New York] (September 30, 1899) 93
47. *The Literary World: A Fortnightly Review of Current Literature* [Boston] (September 30, 1899) 93
48. *The Springfield Republican* [Massachusetts] (November 12, 1899) 94
49. *Detroit Free Press* (November 18, 1899) 94
50. *New-York Tribune (Illustrated Supplement)* (November 19, 1899) 97
51. *The Outlook: A Weekly Review of Politics, Art, Literature, and Finance* [London] (November 25, 1899) 100
52. *The Boston Journal* (November 27, 1899) 100
53. *The San Francisco Wave* (December 9, 1899) 101
54. *The Critic: An Illustrated Monthly Review of Literature, Art and Life* [New York] (December 1899) 103

55. *San Francisco Chronicle* (December 17, 1899).........104
56. *The Annual American Catalogue, 1889*
[New York] (1900) 105
57. *The Brooklyn Daily Eagle* (January 15, 1900)...........105
58. *The Literary World: A Monthly Review of
Current Literature* [Boston] (January 20, 1900)........110
59. *The Times* [Washington] (January 21, 1900)..............110
60. *The Independent* [New York] (January 11, 1900)......113
61. *The National Magazine: An Illustrated American
Monthly* [Boston] (October 1899—March 1900) 113
62. *The New York Times* (March 17, 1900).......................114
63. *Bookseller & Stationer* [Toronto] (May 1900)............115
64. *The New York Times* (May 26, 1900) 115
65. *Bookseller & Stationer* [Toronto] (July 1900) 117
66. *The Literary World* [London] (September 14, 1900) .117
67. *The Literary World* [London] (February 22, 1901)....118
68. *Lloyd's Weekly Newspaper* [London]
(May 12, 1901)..118
69. *The Publishers' Circular and Booksellers'
Record of British and Foreign Literature*
[London] (May 18, 1901)...119
70. *The Queenslander* [Brisbane, Queensland, Australia]
(June 22, 1901)...119
71. *Nelson Evening Mail* [Nelson, New Zealand]
(July 17, 1901) 120
72. *The State* [Columbia, South Carolina]
(August 4, 1901) 121
73. *Longman's Magazine* [London] (October 1901)........122
74. *A Cumulated Index to the Books of 1901*
[Minneapolis] (1902) 124
75. *Detroit Tribune* (January 24, 1902)............................124
76. *The Boston Herald* (April 6, 1902) 125

77. *The Springfield Republican* [Massachusetts] (April 6, 1902) 125

78. *Book News: A Monthly Survey of General Literature* [Philadelphia] (October 1902) 126

79. *The Oxford Point of View* (October 1902) 126

80. *The Augusta Chronicle* [Georgia] (July 9, 1905).......128

81. *The Register* [Adelaide, South Australia] (September 9, 1905)..131

82. *The Sketch* (October 24, 1906).................................133

83. *Marlborough Express* [Blenheim, New Zealand] (November 2, 1909)..133

84. *The Kansas City Star* (September 24, 1911).............133

85. *The Outlook: A Weekly Review of Politics, Art, Literature, and Finance* [London] (1912) 135

86. *The New York Times* (April 26, 1912): 10.................136

87 *The Bookman: A Magazine of Literature and Life* [New York] (June 1912)..136

88. *The Academy and Literature* (June 8, 1912)............138

89. *The Athenaeum* [London] (May 4, 1912)..................138

90. *The New York Herald* (July 6, 1912).........................139

91. *A Guide to the Best Fiction* [New York] (1913) 141

Bibliographical Afterword:
Non-English Editions of *Dracula* 143
J. Gordon Melton

Notes..169

Bibliography..177

For Michael

ACKNOWLEDGMENTS

This volume would not have been complete without the generous help of Elizabeth Miller's *Bram Stoker's Dracula: A Documentary Journey into Vampire Country and the Dracula Phenomenon* (Pegasus, 2009), The Swan River Press, and the blog site *Vampire Over London: Bela Lugosi in Britain* at http://beladraculalugosi.wordpress.com/contemporary-reviews-of-bram-stokers-dracula. I am also deeply indebted to ProQuest and New Statesman Ltd., who generously supplied many of the images reproduced in this volume. The ProQuest images were reproduced from *British Periodicals*. Inquiries may be made to: ProQuest, The Quorum Barnwell Road, Cambridge, CB5 8SW, UK, Tel: +44 (0) 1223 215512, web page: http://www.proquest.co.uk. I am also grateful to the California Digital Newspaper Collection, Center for Bibliographic Studies and Research, University of California, Riverside, who may be contacted at http://cdnc.ucr.edu, to Patrick MacDanel, who generously supplied the cover image for the fourth American edition of *Dracula* (Doubleday, Page & Co., 1902), and to David J. Skal, whose advice and friendship I cherish. Finally, I am indebted to my publisher, John Mabry of Apocryphile Press, whose continued patience and faith in me have made this volume possible.

A NOTE ON THE SELECTIONS AND EDITORIAL PROCEDURE

Some of following selections have been reprinted from other, similar volumes, while the vast majority has been distilled from digitized versions of the original books and journals in which they appeared. The original formatting has been retained as far as possible. Volume, issue, and page number(s) are given where available. Single quotes have been converted to double quotes, where appropriate, and standard British spelling has been maintained, where appropriate. Typographical errors have been silently corrected, and misspellings have been indicated but not corrected.

INTRODUCTION:
THE MYTH OF *DRACULA'S* CRITICAL RECEPTION

John Edgar Browning

"'Dracula' is weird, harrowing, spellbinding, no doubt, to many, but to one who will think and not give up to feeling, it is but an interesting study in the so-called supernatural; not literature in the best sense, with its verisimilitude of faithful chronicling and detective work; and it will, no doubt, "go to storage" along with other books of the times."
—H. M. L., *The Augusta Chronicle* (July 9, 1905)

The only "storage" to which *Dracula* has gone is in the bustling stockrooms of book, film, and video game vendors.

What follows is to date the most exhaustive collection of early critical responses to Bram Stoker's *Dracula* ever assembled. Included are reviews, reactions, and press notices spanning England, Scotland, America, Australia, New Zealand, Canada, and Ireland, the majority of which have not been seen in print since they appeared over 100 years ago. With the exception of The Swan River Press's elegantly hand-crafted pamphlet entitled, *Contemporary Reviews of "Dracula"* (2011), which includes among its contents the not immodest sum of twenty-seven Reviews & Reactions and four different press notices for *Dracula*, the present volume, in which are collected some ninety-one Reviews & Reactions as well as thirty-six different press notices, is able to treat, through sheer greater numbers, *Dracula*'s early critical reception with greater accuracy than any previous

Photograph of Bram Stoker at his craft from The San Francisco Call *(March 13, 1904). (California Digital Newspaper Collection, Center for Bibliographic Studies and Research, University of California, Riverside, http://cdnc.ucr.edu.)*

contemporary analysis has been capable of doing. It is my hope with the present book to lay permanently to rest—as one might a vampire's corpse—a misconception second only to the Vlad/Dracula conundrum.[1] That the sample of reviews relied upon by previous studies about *Dracula*'s publication history is scant at best has unfortunately resulted in the common misconception about the novel's early critical reception being "mixed"— neither completely good nor bad. Building on the pioneering work of *Contemporary Reviews of "Dracula,"*[2] the present work sets out to dispel this myth *en force*. More still, the following reviews will reveal that *Dracula*'s writing was seen by early reviewers and responders to parallel, if not supersede the Gothic horror works of such canonical writers as Mary Shelley, Ann Radcliffe, and Edgar Allan Poe. One reviewer, in fact, calls Stoker the "Edgar Allan Poe of the nineties" (see Review 31).

INTRODUCTION 15

Dracula's early critical history is by and large the product of rumor, one which has over time evolved into fact. An opening passage in the introduction to Clive Leatherdale's annotated edition of Stoker's novel, *Dracula Unearthed* (1988), offers an adequate description of the presently accepted view of *Dracula* as the sensation that almost *wasn't*:

> *Dracula* has trodden an uncertain path these past one hundred years. When Stoker died in 1912, fifteen years after its publication, the book was still in print but otherwise unacclaimed. The best that could be said of it was that *Dracula* was the most successful work of an otherwise second-rate Irish story-teller. And that was not saying much. Indeed, but for one or two quirks of fate, *Dracula* might slowly have slipped into oblivion. That it did not was partly due to revival art forms capitalising on its potential, and partly to an inspired decision taken on the book itself.[3]

Contrary to popular belief, *Dracula* has in truth been, since its inception in the late nineteenth century, the sensation that always *was*. Unfortunately, the general consensus among a great number of studies produced during the last two decades has been that *Dracula* achieved only moderate sales and "mixed" reviews, a perspective which derives largely no doubt from the limited sample of reviews available at the time these studies were produced. And, these studies have, in turn, informed even more secondary works that relied unquestionably upon their predecessors as reliable sources. Interestingly, though, the works that emerged from the initial thrust of writings on *Dracula* during the 1970s generally do not share this claim. Pioneering works like Raymond T. McNally and Radu Florescu's *In Search of Dracula* (1972) and Gabriel Ronay's *The Truth about Dracula* (1972), indeed attest to *Dracula*'s "immediate success"[4] and "instant success...[a work] recognised by fans and critics alike as a horror writer's stroke of genius."[5] Anthony Masters's *The Natural History of the Vampire*

(1972) claims that the novel "immediately achieved enormous popular appeal,"[6] while Basil Copper's *The Vampire in Legend and Fact* (1974) similarly states that *Dracula* was "a phenomenal success."[7] In actuality, the first work to point out any negative remarks by critics seems to have been Harry Ludlam's influential *A Biography of Dracula* (1962), which pre-dates the brunt of the previously given writings by ten years. In it, Ludlam reports that *Dracula* "was released to an astonished press" and "countless...glowing reports...but also some acutely critical."[8] Though Ludlam goes on to list the few negative remarks he was able to locate, he adds that even one in this latter category admits "almost grudgingly" to the accomplishment of Stoker's lurid details.[9] Despite Ludlam's careful handling of the various positive and negative responses (six in all) for which he includes excerpts, unfortunately his biography is probably what supplied the grounds for the myth about *Dracula*'s "mixed" reception.

Daniel Farson reproduces in his biography *The Man Who Wrote Dracula* (1975) many of the "mixed" critical reviews Ludlam's biography had laid out over a decade earlier, but Farson takes the argument one step further by using Ludlam's relatively small sample of reviews as the basis for claiming outright that "though [the novel] was well received, it was not the great success people imagined."[10] Leonard Wolf's pioneering works *A Dream of Dracula* (1972) and *The Annotated Dracula* (1975) make little mention of *Dracula*'s early critical reception,[11] but in his much later work *Dracula: The Connoisseur's Guide* (1997), published to mark the novel's centenary, Wolf offers matter-of-factly that "The reviews of the book were mixed"[12] then proceeds afterwards to excerpt from *The Athenaeum* (see Review 17), *The Spectator* (See Review 26), and *The Bookman* (see Review 28) to substantiate his conclusion.

If we consider the reviews collected here holistically, we find that *Dracula* did not, in fact, receive "mixed reviews" in the general sense. Rather, while the novel did receive, on the one hand, a few reviews that were mixed, it enjoyed predominantly a critically strong early print life. *Dracula* was, by all accounts, a critically-acclaimed novel. To arrive at this conclusion, I employed a very simple system for evaluating and categorizing the reviews and responses containing negative remarks: firstly, generally positive reviews that include perhaps one, sometimes two negative remarks or reservations, of which I have discerned ten examples; secondly, generally mixed reviews in which scorn and praise are relatively balanced, of which I have found four examples[13]; and, thirdly, wholly or mostly negative reviews, of which I managed to locate *only* three examples. What remains are some seventy positive reviews and responses. And, in addition still are thirty-six different laudatory press notices, including: *The Daily Mail, The Daily Telegraph, The Morning Post, Lloyd's weekly Newspaper, Pall Mall Gazette, The Christian World, The Lady, St. Paul's, Bristol Mercury, Lincoln Mercury, Dublin Freeman's Journal, Manchester Courier, Shrewsbury Chronicle, Western Times, Black and White, Birmingham Gazette, Woman, Weekly Liverpool Courier, Punch, Truth, The Morning, The British Weekly, The Referee, Northern Whig, Daily Chronicle, Dundee Advertiser, Sunderland Weekly Echo, The Newsagent, Gloucester Journal, North British Daily Mail, The Speaker, The Literary World, Sheffield Telegraph, Sheffield Independent, Western Times,* and *Oban Times.*

Marvin Kaye aptly refers to the novel, in the introduction to his *Dracula: The Definitive Edition* (1996), as "a late flowering" of the Gothic tradition,[14] but it has become obvious now that *Dracula* is, more precisely, the conclusion to one story and the beginning to another, a sort of hybrid of the vampire "orchids" (*dracula vampira moderna?*) from which every or nearly every vampire narrative for the last century is descended. Many, myself included, have often commented on *Dracula*'s success, both as a novel and a film, as owing much to Stoker's contemporization and modernization of the vampire mythology. Indeed, this sentiment is expressed in a resounding number of the reviews collected here, providing at least some affirmation to our modern perspective. Not only this, contemporary reviews offer incredible insight (aside from the author's own comments, of which there are few) into the contemporary feelings as well as anxieties *Dracula* aroused in the reading public at the *fin de siècle* and in the early twentieth century. It has regularly been the case that the further back we peer into the popular history of Stoker's *Dracula*, the more speculative our conception of the novel's early history really becomes, and the more and more difficult a task it becomes to contextualize accurately *Dracula*'s initial popularity outside the lens of late-twentieth and early-twenty-first century thinking. The reviews collected here offer a more precise alternative to simply inferring much of what we would like to believe. On a similar note, Ludlam offers, and with which I would like to close, that perhaps the only criticism which truly mattered, if only to Stoker himself, are the prophetic words given by Charlotte Stoker, the mother who many decades earlier tended to him as a sickly boy and supplied the stories in which his imaginative vampire *opus* began its gestation:

> "My dear," she wrote from Ireland, "it is splendid, a thousand times beyond anything you have written before, and I feel certain will place you very high in the writers of the day—the story and style being deeply sensational, exciting and interesting." And a few days later she added, "I have seen a great review of 'Dracula' in a London paper. They have not said one word too much of it. No book since Mrs Shelley's 'Frankenstein' or indeed any other at all has come near yours in originality, or terror—Poe is nowhere. I have read much but I never met a book like it at all. In its terrible excitement it should make a widespread reputation and much money for you."[15]

NOTES

[1] See the work of *Dracula* and Bram Stoker scholar Elizabeth Miller.

[2] See Leah Moore and John Reppion, Introduction to *Contemporary Review of "Dracula"* (Dublin: The Swan River Press, 2011), 1-3.

[3] Clive Leatherdale, ed., *Dracula Unearthed* (Westcliff-on-Sea, UK: Desert Island Books, 1988), 7.

[4] Raymond T. McNally and Radu Florescu, *In Search of Dracula: A True History of Dracula and Vampire Legends* (Greenwich, CT: New York Graphic Society Ltd., 1972), 162.

[5] Gabriel Ronay, *The Truth about Dracula* (New York: Stein and Day, 1974 [1972]), 53.

[6] Anthony Masters, *The Natural History of the Vampire* (New York: G.P Putnam's Sons, 1972), 208.

[7] Basil Copper, *The Vampire in Legend and Fact* (Secaucus, NJ: The Citadel Press, 1974), 74.

[8] Harry Ludlam, *A Biography of Dracula: The Life Story of Bram Stoker* (London: W. Foulsham & Co., 1962), 107.

[9] *Ibid.*, 108.

[10] Daniel Farson, *The Man Who Wrote Dracula: A Biography of Bram Stoker* (London: Michael Joseph, 1975), 162-163.

[11] See Leonard Wolf, *A Dream of Dracula: In Search of the Living Dead* (New York: Little, Brown, 1972) and (ed.) *The Annotated Dracula* (New York: Clarkson N. Potter, Inc., 1975).

[12] Leonard Wolf, *Dracula: The Connoisseur's Guide* (New York: Broadway Books, 1997), 141.

[13] I should also note here that many of the "negative" remarks or reservations in this category reference Stoker's novel as having succeeded in frightening the reviewer *too* much and thus could not be recommended by the reviewer for "sensitive persons."

[14] Marvin Kaye, ed., Introduction to *Dracula: The Definitive Edition* (Barnes & Noble Books, 1996), x.

[15] Ludlam, *A Biography of Dracula*, 108-109.

REVIEWS & REACTIONS

1. THE DAILY NEWS [LONDON] (MAY 27, 1897): 6.

MR. BRAM STOKER'S NEW STORY

What has become of the "general decay of faith" of which Parson Holmes reproachfully discoursed at Francis Allen's that night when the poet read aloud his fragment "Morte d'Arthur", the noble precursor of *The Idylls of the King*? Have old beliefs really ceased to impress the imagination? It may be so; but our novelists are clearly experiencing a reawakened faith in the charm of the supernatural. Here, for the latest example, is Mr. Bram Stoker taking in hand the old-world legend of the Were-wolf[1] or vampire, with all its weird and exciting associations of blood-sucking and human flesh devouring, and interweaving it with the threads of a long story with an earnestness, a directness, and a simple good faith which ought to go far to induce readers of fiction to surrender their imaginations into the novelist's hands. Of course the secret lies here. The story writer who would make others believe must himself believe, or learn at least to write as if he did. There must be no display of meaningless rhetoric, no selection of faded terrors out of the dusty scene-docks of the suburban theatres. The more strange the facts, the more businesslike should be the style and method of narration. Some there be who, in handling such themes, prefer to take shelter in a remote time; but the supernatural which cannot stand the present day, and even the broad daylight of the world around us, stands at half confessed imposture. Mr. Stoker has not been unmindful of these canons of the art of the weird novel writer. His story is told in sections, in the form of letters or excerpts from diaries of the various personages, which is in itself a straightforward proceeding, investing the whole narrative with a documentary air. Ships' logs and medical practitioners' notebooks of cases also come in aid, with now and then a matter-of-fact extract from the columns of our contemporaries, *The Westminster* and *The Pall Mall Gazette,* about mysterious crimes attributed to an unseen destroyer popularly known as "the Bloofer lady", the victims of whom are mostly little children

Cover for the first edition of Dracula
(Archibald Constable & Co., 1897).

whose throats are found marked with two little punctures, such as of old were believed to be made by the "Vampire Bat", who lives on human blood. These details are not the mere background of the story; for the mysteries of Lycanthropy, once devoutly believed in throughout Europe and the east, permeate the whole narrative and give their peculiar colouring to the web of romance with which they are associated. The author's artistic instincts have rightly suggested that the first step must be to attune the mind of the reader to the key of the story, for which purpose nothing could be more effective than the opening chapters, which are given up to the journal kept in shorthand by the hero, Jonathan Harker, the young solicitor who, leaving his fiancee, Mina Murray, behind in

England, starts on a mission connected with the purchase of some estates and an ancient manor house in this country to the mysterious Count Dracula, a Transylvanian nobleman, who lives in a lonely castle in the Carpathians. The long drive from Buda-Pesth is graphically described, while a constantly-growing sense of some vague impending trouble is cleverly made to intensify the interest and curiosity of the reader. Sometimes it is the strange, anxious glances of innkeepers and attendants, who know that the traveller is on the way to sojourn at the Count's gloomy and almost inaccessible abode; at others it is a word let fall, which, though in Serbian or Slovak language, conveys to the mind of the traveller a sinister idea. One worthy old landlady at a post-house puts a rosary around her guest's neck, reminding him that it is the eve of St. George's Day, when at midnight all evil things have full sway, and after vainly imploring him to consider where he is going and what he is going to, places for protection a rosary around his neck. Even the crowd about the inn doors share in the worthy hostess's solicitude:

> When we started, the crowd round the inn door, which had by this time swelled to a considerable size, all made the sign of the Cross and pointed two fingers towards me. With some difficulty I got a fellow-passenger to tell me what they meant; he would not answer at first, but on learning that I was English he explained that it was a charm or guard against the evil eye. This was not very pleasant for me, just starting for an unknown place to meet an unknown man; but every one seemed so kind-hearted, and so sorrowful, and so sympathetic that I could not but be touched. I shall never forget the last glimpse which I had of the inn-yard and its crowd of picturesque figures, all crossing themselves, as they stood round the wide archway, with its background of rich foliage of oleander and orange trees in green tubs clustered in the centre of the

ARCHIBALD CONSTABLE & CO.'s LIST.

AT ALL LIBRARIES, BOOKSELLERS', AND BOOKSTALLS.

IN the TIDEWAY. By Flora Annie Steel. 6s.
The FOLLY of PEN HARRINGTON. By Julian Sturgis. 6s.
The AMAZING MARRIAGE. By George Meredith. 6s.
DRACULA. By Bram Stoker. 6s.
GREEN FIRE. By Fiona Macleod. 6s.
SELECTED POEMS. By George Meredith. 6s. net.
NEW POEMS. By Francis Thompson. 6s. net.
The OBSERVATIONS of a FOSTER PARENT. By John Charles Tarver.
An ENGLISH GARNER. By Professor Edward Arber. Vol. VIII. now ready, 5s. net.
POPULAR RELIGION and FOLK-LORE in NORTHERN INDIA. By William Crooke. Illustrated.
2 vols, 21s. net.
The PREACHING of ISLAM. By T. W. Arnold. Demy 8vo. 12s.
ENGLISH SCHOOLS, 1546-1548. By A. F. Leach. Demy 8vo. 12s. net.
WHITMAN : a Study. By John Burroughs. 6s. net.
An ESSAY on COMEDY, and The USES of the COMIC SPIRIT. By George Meredith. 5s. net.
The CHRONICLE of VILLANI. A Book for Dante Students. Translated by Rose E. Selfe.
Edited by P. H. WICKSTEED. 6s.
HAROLD. By Lord Lytton. Edited by J. Laurence Gomme. 3s. 6d.
A WRITER of FICTION. By Chris Holland, Author of ' My Japanese Wife.' 2s. 6d.
The LOVE of an OBSOLETE WOMAN. 2s. 6d.
IMPERIAL DEFENCE. By Sir Charles Dilke and Spenser Wilkinson. New Edition. 2s. 6d.
The GAME of POLO. By T. F. Dale. 21s. net.
The NATION'S AWAKENING. By Spenser Wilkinson. 3s. 6d.
SONGS of the MAID. By John Huntley Skrine. 5s.
SONGS and MEDITATIONS. By Maurice Hewlett. 5s.
SONGS for LITTLE PEOPLE. By Norman Gale. Illustrated by Helen Stratton. 6s.
The STORY of an AFRICAN CRISIS and the JAMESON RAID. Illustrated. By F. E. Garrett,
Editor of the Cape Times. 3s. 6d.
BOSWELL'S LIFE of JOHNSON. Edited by Augustine Birrell. With Frontispieces. 6 vols.
fcap. 8vo. cloth, paper label, or gilt extra. 2s. net per Volume; also half-morocco, 3s. net per Volume. Sold in Sets only.

CONSTABLE'S REPRINT OF THE WAVERLEY NOVELS.
THE FAVOURITE EDITION OF SIR WALTER SCOTT.
With all the Original Plates and Vignettes (Re-engraved). In Forty-eight Volumes.
Fcap. 8vo. cloth, paper label title, 1s. 6d. net per Volume, or 3l. 12s. the Set. Also cloth gilt, gilt top, 2s. net per Volume, or 4l. 16s. the Set ;
and half-leather gilt, 2s. 6d. net per Volume, or 6l. the Set.

ARCHIBALD CONSTABLE & CO. 2, Whitehall-gardens, Westminster.

Constable ad from The Athanaeum, *no. 3628 (May 8, 1897): 632. (Image published with permission of ProQuest and New Statesman Ltd. Further reproduction is prohibited without permission.)*

yard. Then our driver, whose wide linen drawers covered the whole front of the box-seat—"gotza," they call them—cracked his big whip over his four small horses, which ran abreast, and we set off on our journey. I soon lost sight and recollection of ghostly fears in the beauty of the scene as we drove along, although had I known the language, or rather languages, which my fellow passengers were speaking, I might not have been able to throw them off so easily.

Strange, unearthly experiences indeed are in store for the young traveller in the chateau of the Count before this opening, which may be regarded as the prologue of the story, is concluded; but interest in a narrative whose effect depends so much on the feeling of curiosity must not be forestalled. For details, therefore, of how Jonathan Harker finally escaped from the castle and its terrible inmates to the shelter of a friendly convent in Buda-Pesth, where he is found by the faithful Mina suffering from brain fever; and also for the more marvellous incidents after their return to England which form the chief substance of the narrative, we must send the reader to Mr. Bram Stoker's volume. Few stories recently published have been more rich in sensations or in the Websterian power of "moving a horror" by subtle suggestion.

✳ ✳ ✳

2. LLOYD'S WEEKLY NEWSPAPER [LONDON], NO. 2845 (MAY 30, 1897): 8.

A ROMANCE OF VAMPIRISM

Without doubt Mr. Bram Stoker has given us one of the weirdest romances of late years in his present book. As the basis of his story he has taken the most gruesome superstition that ever haunted the mind of man, yet one that is fall of immense possibilities to the writer of fiction, and of these he has made the most. Shortly, Vampirism, as described by Calmont[2] *[sic]* and other writers on the subject, is a belief that certain persons during life are imbued with an overpowering desire to suck the blood of living creatures, especially human beings. The practice changes them to semi-demons, and after death the corpse, instead of putrefying, retains the hues of health, and every night the astral form, as the Theosophists might term it, rises from its grave a vampire, seeking to suck the blood of some living person, thereby fattening the corpse as it lies in its coffin, the persons so bitten and sucked becoming at death themselves vampires. The present story begins with the diary of a solicitor's clerk, sent into Transylvania to interview a mysterious Count Dracula, who has purchased property in England. Dracula is not only a vampire, but the chief of vampires, possessing miraculous powers over wolves and other wild creatures; and the experiences of Jonathan Harker, the clerk in question, are weird in the extreme. Then the vampire count comes to England, and other writers take up the story, which is woven together in a masterly fashion that irresistibly reminds one of the late Wilkie Collins. To the rescue of those who have fallen under the spell of this mediaeval terror let loose again to work its wicked will in the latter days of the nineteenth century comes an old German[3] *[sic]* scientist, one Van Helsing, with whom the reader will at once be charmed. In the end he, with the help of an English mad-doctor Dr. Seward, prevails, and the demon is vanquished. By no means can this be sailed a cheerful book, but it is one nevertheless, that most readers will peruse with intense interest, held to the end by that peculiar fascination which all supernatural subjects invariably excite in the human mind when they are treated by a writer who wields a vivid pen. Throughout the work, from a literary point of view, is of the highest character. Mr. Stoker has started with the tacit assumption that the horrible creatures he describes do really exist, and by so doing he shows that he has grasped the true spirit of all romance. The weirdness of the subject cannot fail to attract attention, and the manner in which the author has worked out his story, and made the strange old superstition such a seemingly possible factor in latter-day life[4] is certain to add considerably to his reputation.

***

3. THE DAILY MAIL
[LONDON] (JUNE 1, 1897): 3.

It is said of Mrs. Radcliffe that, when writing her now almost forgotten romances, she shut herself up in absolute seclusion, and fed upon raw beef, in order to give her work the desired atmosphere of gloom, tragedy and terror. If one had no assurance to the contrary, one might well suppose that a similar method and regimen had been adopted by Mr. Bram Stoker while writing his new novel *Dracula*. In seeking for a parallel to this weird, powerful, and horrorful story our mind reverts to such tales as *The Mysteries of Udolpho, Frankenstein, Wuthering Heights, The Fall of the House of Usher,* and *Margery of Quether.* But *Dracula* is even more appalling in its gloomy fascination than any one of these.

We started reading it early in the evening, and followed Jonathan Harker on his mission to the Carpathians with no definite conjecture as to what awaited us in the castle of Dracula. When we came to the night journey over the mountain road and were chased by the wolves, which the driver, with apparently miraculous power, repelled by a mere gesture,[5] we began to scent mystery, but were not perturbed. The first thrill of horrible sensation came with the discovery that the driver and Count Dracula were one and the same person, that the Count was the only human inhabitant of the castle, and that the rats, the bats, the ghosts, and the howling wolves were his familiars.

By ten o'clock the story had so fastened itself upon our attention that we could not pause even to light our pipe. At midnight the narrative had fairly got upon our nerves; a creepy terror had seized upon us, and when at length, in the early hours of the morning, we went upstairs to bed it was with the anticipation of nightmare. We listened anxiously for the sound of bats' wings against the window; we even felt at our throat in dread lest an actual vampire should have left there the two ghastly punctures which in Mr. Stoker's book attested to the hellish operations of Dracula.[6]

The recollection of this weird and ghostly tale will doubtless haunt us for some time to come. It would be unfair to the author to divulge the plot. We therefore restrict ourselves to the statement that the eerie chapters are written and strung together with very considerable art and cunning, and also with unmistakable literary power. Tribute must also be paid to the rich imagination of which Mr. Bram Stoker here gives liberal evidence. Persons of small courage and weak nerves should confine their reading of these gruesome pages strictly to the hours between dawn and sunset.

✻ ✻ ✻

4. PALL MALL GAZETTE [LONDON] (JUNE 1, 1897): 11.

FOR MIDNIGHT READING

Mr. Bram Stoker should have labelled his book "For Strong Men Only", or words to that effect. Left lying carelessly around, it might get into the hands of your maiden aunt, who believes devoutly in the man under the bed, or of the new parlour maid with unsuspected hysterical tendencies. *Dracula* to such would be manslaughter. It is for the man with a sound conscience and digestion, who can turn out the gas and go to bed without having to look over his shoulder more than half a dozen times as he goes upstairs, or more than mildly wishing that he had a crucifix and some garlic handy to keep the vampires from getting at him. That is to say, the story deals with the Vampire King, and it is horrid and creepy to the last degree. It is also excellent, and one of the best things in the supernatural line that we have been lucky enough to hit upon. To expound the story in any detail would be grossly unfair to Mr. Bram Stoker, besides being utterly impossi-

DRACULA

By BRAM STOKER, *Author of "The Shoulder of Shasta,"*
"The Watter's Mou'," etc.

"In seeking a parallel to *this weird, powerful, and horrorful story,* our mind reverts to such tales as 'The Mysteries of Udolpho,' 'Frankenstein,' 'Wuthering Heights,' 'The Fall of the House of Usher,' and 'Marjery of Quether.' But 'Dracula' is even more *appalling in its gloomy fascination* than any one of these."
—*The Daily Mail.*

"'Dracula' is one of the most weird and spirit-quelling romances which have appeared for years. . . . The reader hurries on breathless from the first page to the last, afraid to miss a single word, lest the subtle and complicated chain of evidence should be broken. . . . And though the plot involves enough and to spare of bloodshed, it never becomes revolting, because the spiritual mystery of evil continually surmounts the physical horror."—*The Daily Telegraph.*

"It would be difficult to meet in any recent novel with finer pages of descriptive writing."—*The Morning Post.*

"The story is woven together in a masterly fashion. Most readers will peruse it with intense interest throughout. The work, from a literary point of view, is of the highest character."—*Lloyd's Weekly Newspaper,* May 30, 1897.

"It is horrid and creepy to the last degree. It is also excellent, and one of the best things in the supernatural line that we have been lucky enough to hit upon. . . . Having once got through the first half-dozen pages, every one will finish the rest in as few sittings as possible. . . . This is a book to revel in. We did it ourselves, and we are not ashamed to say so."—*Pall Mall Gazette,* June 1, 1897.

Press notices for Dracula from Odd Stories
(Archibald Constable & Co., 1897): 319.

ble, owing to the mass of corroborative detail and the tremendous complications, which, however, can be followed without a headache. It opens with the journey of a solicitor's clerk into the heart of the Carpathians, where the terror of the peasantry indicates that he is likely to meet with something uncommon. He does, and that something is—Dracula. Having once got through the first half-dozen pages, every one will finish the rest in as few sittings as possible, and, for reasons given above, we decline to tell what that rest is. It is enough to say that Mr. Bram Stoker has mastered the real secrets of a genuine "creep". A glance at your pipe-rack and evening paper will not save you, for Mr. Bram Stoker lays the main scenes of his tale in England and London, right up to date, with the type-writer, the phonograph, the *Pall Mall Gazette,* the Zoo, and all the latest improvements complete. That is the way to make a horror convincing. The mediaeval is well enough in its way, but you don't care what sort of bogeys troubled your ancestors all that way back. And, again, Mr. Stoker understands how to sustain the interest. He gives you drops into the lifelike commonplace, which, nevertheless, tell upon the plot;

REVIEWS & REACTIONS   31

and he sandwiches the various sides of his story in together at intervals of a few pages by means of an ingenious collection of diaries, newspaper extracts, &c, in chronological order. There are slight discrepancies, possibly, and the mechanism which helps the characters out is once or twice rather too obviously mechanism; but that is inevitable. And there is a creep in every dozen pages or so. For those who like that, this is a book to revel in. We did it ourselves, and are not ashamed to say so.

* * *

5. THE BOOKSELLERS' REVIEW
[LONDON] 13 (JUNE 3, 1897): 169.

This is an exciting story from beginning to finish. True, it is very largely made up from diaries and phonographs, but it all pieces out very well and makes a pleasing whole, with the air of mystery which the reader is always endeavouring to probe.

The novel opens with a solicitor on his way to Transylvania, to visit a Count who lives in one of those secluded castles so peculiar to Transylvania. You see them perched away on the top of an apparently inaccessible rock, and they are only approached by a most circuitous and perpendicular road. There are no end of adventures both without and within the castle; a pack of wolves is met on the way, and are only dispersed by the aid of some agency that isn't human; within the castle the Count betrays many eccentricities in the way of climbing up the front of his castle, like an animal of the lower creation. The solicitor's adventures are rather blood curdling, but at length he escapes from his unpleasant host to a convent, where he is attacked with brain fever. The volume is packed full of gruesome horrors and marvellous experience, and those who like that sort of thing will find it to their heart's content.

6. THE DAILY TELEGRAPH
[LONDON] (JUNE 3, 1897): 6.

BOOKS OF THE DAY

Romance is dying—according to some *litterateur,* who seems to think that perennial forms of human thought are as transitory as fashion. Already the public is getting tired of romance, and is once more asking for the social problems and the deeper analysis into character which were temporarily obscured by the extravagances of the New Woman. It is odd that, under circumstances like these, one of the most curious and striking of recent productions should be a revival of a mediaeval superstition, the old legend of the "were-wolf", as illustrated and modernised by Mr. Bram Stoker, in the book which he entitles *Dracula.* For there are two things which are remarkable in the novel—the first is the confident reliance on superstition as furnishing the groundwork of a modern story; and the second, more significant still, is the bold adaptation of the legend to such ordinary spheres of latter-day existence as the harbour of Whitby and Hampstead Heath.[7] What is the good of telling us that romance is dead, or dying, when we see before our eyes its triumph and survival in ghost stories from the Highlands, and the scientific mysticism of the Psychical Society? How absurd to suppose that even the old gloomy and awe-inspiring melodrama of *The Castle of Otranto* has disappeared when Mr. Bram Stoker invites us to sup on horrors, not only in the Carpathian Mountains, but in the more cheerful and commonplace precincts of our metropolis! Superstition, whether we view it from the standpoint of folk-lore or in the shape in which it appealed to Dickens's fat boy, is apparently the deathless accompaniment of civilisation. It is not only the savage and barbarian who likes to feel his flesh creep; it is the fashionable man or woman at the end of a century, who, sceptical of almost everything else, becomes anxious at the spilling of salt, and refuses to sit down at a table of thirteen.

REVIEWS & REACTIONS

Dracula, at all events, is one of the most weird and spirit-quelling romances which have appeared for years. It begins in a masterly fashion in the wilds of Transylvania, and introduces to us an ordinary solicitor's clerk, engaged on a mission to a Count who lives in its most remote fastnesses. How is it that in his progress to his destination the air seems to be full of omens? Why is it that the simple villagers at Bistritz press upon him branches of garlic and rosaries? Because it is the doom of Mr. Jonathan Harker, solicitor's clerk to Mr. Hawkins, to have to see a man-wolf, a Count Dracula, who from sunset to sunrise satisfies his thirst for human blood under appalling circumstances of secrecy and horror. Here is a commencement which lacks no element of the uncanny and the gruesome. We are at home in that precise corner of Europe which shelters the superstitions of the Middle Ages: we feel that anything can happen in the midst of the Carpathian Mountains,[8] and Castle Dracula may be situated anywhere we please within the region which is the wildest and least known portion of the Continent. All the better if the narrator of the tale be nothing more or less than a solicitor's clerk. It is the juxtaposition of the ordinary with the supernatural which gives the latter its significance. We accept the wildest adventures because the man who experienced them was only plain Mr. Jonathan Harker, engaged to Miss Mina Murray in England.[9]

Were-wolf, Lycanthrope, Loup-garou—the name was familiar enough in Europe some centuries ago. The idea that a man can turn himself into a wolf begins early in recorded literature; we remember the story of Lycaon in Ovid's "Metamorphoses" and the noted wizard Moeris in Virgil's "Ecologues," who by the aid of Pontic poisons hid himself in the woods, and could bring the ghosts of dead men from their sepulchres. What has Mr. Bram Stoker been reading?[10] Has he got hold of Richard Verstegan, who tells us in 1605 that it was a common thing in England for certain savage men to change at night time into wolves, and traverse the country seeking whom they could devour? Or is his authority Mr. Baring-Gould, who, in 1865, published "The Book of Were-Wolves," together with every kind of rationalistic and perhaps not very convincing explanation that some specimens of the human race were born with a thirst for human blood? I seem also to remember that Mr. G. W. M. Reynolds, who posed as a Chartist some twenty or thirty years ago, and varied the task of founding *Reynolds's Newspaper* by addressing a crowd of homeless vagabonds on the iniquities of the income-tax, wrote a "London Journal" story on the were-wolf. At all events, history tells us that late in the sixteenth century a man called Gilles Garnier was arrested at Dôle, in France, on the charge of being a man-wolf, and that one of the means whereby human creatures could thus metamorphose themselves was a girdle of wolf-skin which they clasped around their loins. Naturally enough, however, the superstition was only prevalent so long as wolves themselves existed in the various countries. In England, for instance, James I can tell us in his "Demonologie" that the old legend is an absurd one, while as a matter of fact, it is not the wolf but the black cat, as a more familiar animal, which serves in our own country as the mystic instrument of witch-like juggleries. Not always is the wolf himself accepted in tradition as a destroying agency. It is true that in the shape of a grandmother he does his best to devour Little Red Riding-hood, but Rome owes it to a wolf that Romulus ever existed, and some forms of the story of "Beauty and the Beast" make the future husband of the beautiful heroine a wolf-like animal, susceptible to the fascination of flowers. Perhaps the were-wolf was in reality a metaphorical figure for the outlaw, the man who preferred a vendetta to all kinds of money composition for injuries, a man with a price set on his head as an enemy to society, whom at all hazards a developing civilisation had to destroy.

All this doubtless, Mr. Bram Stoker is familiar with, but it leads to a point which concerns the mechanism of his tale. After Mr. Harker's episode in Transylvania, and his escape from the castle of Count Dracula, the story changes to Whitby, and we discover a fresh arena for the maleficent energies of the were-wolf. The Count has purchased a little property in England, for no other reason than the desire to extend the range of his operations. Nor is his success less extraordinary than his nature. He infects with wolf-madness the body of Miss Lucy Westenra, engaged to Mr. Arthur Holmwood, and is the immediate cause of her melancholy demise. He makes a wolf desert the safe precincts of the Zoological Gardens and range at large for the express edification of the contemporary newspaper reporter. He fills the mad soul of a patient named Renfield with a lust for devouring flies and spiders, before aiming at higher game. Science is powerless before him. An Amsterdam specialist, Van Helsing, conspires with Dr. Seward to defeat his purposes, but these lights of modern knowledge have to fall back on the simpler remedies of garlic, crucifix, and consecrated wafer, and abjure the refinements of medical and pathological analysis. Poor Lucy Westenra, dead to human eyes, haunts the suburban heights of Hampstead and purloins the wandering children in the northern regions of the metropolis. Only when the wife of Jonathan Harker is herself tainted with the wolf poison can Van Helsing, Dr. Seward, Holmwood, and Quincey Morris succeed in tracking the monster to his lair. Count Dracula is killed at last before the sun reaches the horizon, and the world is once more at rest. Never was so mystical a tale told with such simple verisimilitude. We are not allowed to doubt the facts because the author speaks of them as mere matters of ascertained truth. Such is Mr. Stoker's dramatic skill, that the reader hurries on breathless from the first page to the last, afraid to miss a single word, the subtle and complicated chain of evidence should be broken; and though the plot involves enough and to spare of bloodshed, it never becomes revolting, because the spiritual mystery of evil continually surmounts the physical horror.

Nevertheless, there is no part of the book so good as the opening section. The reason is obvious. In telling a tale of romantic mystery the atmosphere, the mise-en-scene, the local colouring, are quite as important as the central incidents. When you are transported to an unknown region everything is possible. But the Château en Espagne—or, for the matter of that, the Castle in the Carpathian mountains—must not be transferred to the home of the railway and the phonograph. Besides, the legend of the were-wolf died in England when the wolf ceased to be a formidable enemy; it died, too, even in France after the end of the sixteenth century. There is yet another point which is a little confusing to the ordinary reader. The mechanism of thaumaturgy must always be rational, however ideal and supernatural may be the story. We resent the notion that a man or woman can be turned into a wolf, unless he or she has shown wolf-like propensities. What had Lucy Westenra done that her pure soul should be contaminated? Or Mina Harker, that she should be forced to drink Count Dracula's blood? Renfield we understand, because he was a madman; but if goodness can be turned into vice by a purely extraneous agency, the mystery of evil becomes too awful for us to contemplate. According to the older idea, this particular transformation was accomplished by Satanic agency, voluntarily submitted to because of an innate craving for human flesh. Macbeth could not have been tempted by the witches if he had not already conceived wicked schemes of ambition, nor could Faust have listened to the counsels of Mephistopheles if his own mind had not been infected with recrudescent passion. Such, at least, is our modern ethical principle, which we are loath to relinquish even in dealing with the sphere of transcendental mystery.

—*W. L. Courtney*

✳ ✳ ✳

7. THE BRISTOL TIMES AND MIRROR 126, NO. 10142 (JUNE 5, 1897): 13.

DRACULA. By Bram Stoker. We must confess at the outset that we are not particularly fond of novels cast in diary form. But Mr Bram Stoker explains that these papers have been placed in sequence, and that how this has been done will be manifest to the reader as he proceeds. Jonathan Harker's journal sets forth, in the first place, his quest for Castle Dracula. The district he had to travel "is in the extreme east of the country, just on the borders of

BITS FROM BOOKS REVIEWED IN THIS NUMBER

A Ghostly Count.

I had hung my shaving glass by the window and was just beginning to shave. Suddenly I felt a hand on my shoulder, and heard the Count's voice saying to me, "Good-morning." I started, for it amazed me that I had not seen him, since the reflection of the glass covered the whole room behind me. In starting I had cut myself slightly, but did not notice it at the moment. Having answered the Count's salutation, I turned to the glass again to see how I had been mistaken. This time there could be no error, for the man was close to me and I could see him over my shoulder. But there was no reflection of him in the mirror! . . . . I laid down the razor, turning as I did so half round to look for some sticking plaster. When the Count saw my face his eyes blazed with a sort of demoniac fury, and he suddenly made a grab at my throat. I drew away, and his hand touched the string of beads which held the crucifix. It made an instant change in him, for the fury passed so quickly that I could hardly believe it was ever there.

"Dracula." By Bram Stoker.

"A Ghostly Count," excerpt of Dracula *from* The Booksellers' Review, *no. 13 (June 3, 1897): 170.*

three States, Transylvania, Moldavia, and Bukovina, in the midst of the Carpathian Mountains, one of the wildest and least known portions of Europe. I was not able to light on any map or work giving me exact locality of the Castle Dracula, as there are no maps of the country as yet, but I found that Bistritz, the post-town named by count Dracula, is a fairly well-known place." The author gives us some graphic sketches of the country and its people, and shortly receives a hearty welcome from Count Dracula to his "beautiful land." But Count was a mystery. When the landlord was asked by the traveller if he knew Count Dracula, "and could tell me anything of his castle, both he and his wife crossed themselves, and, saying they knew nothing at all, simply refused to speak further. It was so near the time of starting that I had no time to ask anyone else, for it was all very mysterious and not by any means comforting." Jonathan Harker's account of his approach to the castle is very powerfully told, but we feel as we read it that we are getting deeper and deeper into a land of shadows, weird and uncanny. A further acquaintance with Count Dracula certainly does not daunt the mystery which hangs about that person. We wish we had space to quote the very clever piece of writing which reveals to the reader the fact that Jonathan Harker, the bearer of the sealed letter from Hawkins, and Count Dracula were the only inhabitants of the castle, "I have only the Count to speak with, and he—I fear I am myself the only living soul within the place. Let me be prosaic so far as facts can be. It will help me to bear up, and imagination must not run riot with me. If it does I am lost." To those who are fond of the ghastly and gruesome, "Dracula" will be welcome reading. The story is cleverly constructed and brilliantly told, and we do not think we can add further praise to the manner in which Mr Bram Stoker sets forth the mysterious and the awful—London: Archibald Constable and Co. 2 Whitehall gardens.

※ ※ ※

8. THE GLASGOW HERALD
(JUNE 10, 1897): 10.

It is an eerie and gruesome tale which Mr. Stoker tells, but it is much the best book he has written. The reader is held with a spell similar to that of Wilkie Collins's *Moonstone,* and indeed in many ways the form of narrative by diaries and letters and extracts from newspapers neatly fitted into each other recalls Wilkie Collins's style. Mr. Stoker's story begins in Transylvania, where a young English solicitor goes to take the instructions of Count Dracula as to an English estate which he has purchased. The solicitor's adventures in the remote castle at first are simply interesting; shortly they become horrible, for in the mysterious Dracula he finds one who is neither more nor less than a vampire, who dies daily and rises at night to gorge himself upon human bodies, who can creep up and down his outside walls like a lizard, and who has a hundred other fearful and blood-curdling peculiarities. When we have supped full of Transylvanian horrors, the author skilfully shifts the scene to England, where the appearance of Dracula, first in one locality and then in another, causes misery and terror to two or three households, which are exceedingly well imagined. Mr. Stoker keeps his devilry well in hand, if such an expression is allowable; as strange event follows strange event, the narrative might in less skilful hands become intolerably improbable; but *Dracula* to the end seems only too reasonably and sanely possible. Henceforth we shall wreathe ourselves in garlic when opportunity offers, and firmly decline all invitations to visit out-of-the-way clients in castles in the South-East of Europe. *Dracula* is a first rate book of adventure.

※ ※ ※

9. THE SPEAKER
[LONDON] (JUNE 12, 1897): 662.

DRACULA. BY BRAM STOKER.
LONDON: ARCHIBALD CONSTABLE & CO.

MR. BRAM STOKER, in his remarkable novel "Dracula," has gone to the old legends of the were-wolf for the inspiration of his story. For some reason unknown, Transylvania and the more remote districts of the Bukovina have been accepted by general consent as the home of these traditions. It is only, apparently, in the neighborhood of the Carpathians that the were-wolf is permitted to flourish. Mr. Stoker begins his story in orthodox fashion in a lonely Carpathian castle, and gives us a thrilling narrative of the terrible experiences of Mr. Jonathan Harker, a young English solicitor, in that abode of mystery. But having struck the keynote of his story in this fashion, our author makes a bold departure, and at a single stroke transfers the were-wolf from Hungary to England, where he is seen sojourning, not only on the coast of Yorkshire, but in the very streets of London itself. It is a daring thing that has been thus attempted by Mr. Stoker, and he may fairly be congratulated upon the success of his achievement. That success is all the greater inasmuch as he has allowed himself to be hampered by the method in which he tells his story. That he is a master of straightforward narrative is proved by the four chapters with which the story opens. He has chosen, however, to adopt the methods of the late Mr. Wilkie Collins, and to give us his weird and powerful story in the shape of a series of narratives by different persons, and of extracts from diaries kept by different hands. It says much for his command of his gruesome theme that in spite of being thus handicapped in his methods he has succeeded in making his story intensely interesting. It is not, of course, a story which can be commended to readers with weak nerves. The author has not spared us in his description of the horrors with which tradition has invested the legend of the were-wolf, and the portrait he gives us of the mysterious and terrible Count Dracula, who commands the secrets of the charnel-house, and wooes men and women to their eternal undoing, may cause some readers the unpleasant sensations of a nightmare. But those who are not afraid of the strong meat of this description will find "Dracula" to be a story of very real power, told with remarkable skill and with unflagging spirit. The supernatural element is managed with great dexterity and an appearance of realism that is extremely ingenious. Upon the whole, as the first introduction of the were-wolf to English soil, "Dracula" must be pronounced a distinct success.

✻ ✻ ✻

10. THE ACADEMY: A WEEKLY REVIEW OF LITERATURE, SCIENCE, AND ART (FICTION SUPPLEMENT) [LONDON], NO. 1310 (JUNE 12, 1897): 11.

Dracula. By Bram Stoker. (Constable & Co.) Anyone, I think, who has watched with any attention the tendencies of recent fiction will have noted an increasing taste for what I may call "horrors." One sees the same thing, of course, in journalism. Crimes, floods, fires, "horrid details" of all kinds sell more editions of an evening paper than far more important and edifying matters. Many of the magazines, too, seemed to rely on attracting readers by stories that are gruesome or revolting rather than by more cheerful reading. That the tendency is a particularly good one I cannot venture to assert, but it exists and must be taken into account. Mr. Bram Stoker's new book, *Dracula*, is an example of this school of work. The story is one long nightmare, full of madhouse imaginings, vampires, and everything that is likely to keep nervous people from sleep at night. It is a curious compound of realism and sensationalism; but though it does not belong to a school that I admire, it is written at times with considerable power. The descriptions of count Dracula's Transylvanian castle, and, indeed, the whole picture of Jonathan Harker's experiences in the Carpathians, are done with a vivid impressionist touch which strikes home at once to the imagination, while the supernatural element of horror is so skillfully worked in the earlier chapters as to be, for the moment, quite convincing. Here is an effective passage:

> At last there came a time when the driver went further afield than she had yet gone, and gearing his absence the horses began to tremble worse than ever, and to snort and scream with fright. I could not see any cause for it, for the howling of the walls had ceased altogether; but just then the moon, sailing through the black clouds, appeared behind the jagged crest of a beetling, pine-clad rock, and by its light I saw around us a ring of wolves, with white teeth and lolling red tongues, with long sinewy limbs and shaggy hair. They were hundred times more terrible in the grim silence which held them than even when they howled. For myself I felt a sort of paralysis of fear. It is only when a man feels himself face-to-face with such horrors that he can understand their true import.

The middle part of the book, where the scene is mainly in England, strikes me as less good. Vampires need a Transylvanian background to be convincing.[11] The witches in "Macbeth" would not be effective in Oxford-Street. And Mr. Stoker's method of telling his story by extracts from different peoples diaries, letters, and the like unduly prolongs the book and makes the incidents less easy to follow. He is best in his most nightmarish mood.

> I knew that there were at least three graves to find—graves that are inhabit; so I search, and search, and I find one of them. She lay in her vampire sleep, so full of life and voluptuous beauty that I shudder as though I have come to do murder. Ah, I doubt not that in old time, when

such things were, many a man who set forth to do such a task as mine found at the last his heart fail him, and then his nerve! So he delay, and delay, till the mere beauty and the fascination of the wanton Un-dead have hypnotise him; and he remain on and on till sunset come, and the vampire sleep the over. Then the beautiful eyes of the fair woman open and look love, and the voluptuous mouth present to a kiss—and man is weak.

The speaker is Dr. Van Helsing, which accounts for the curious English. I have written enough, I think, to show my readers what to expect from *Dracula*. If they want their flesh to be made to "creep" Mr. Stoker will be able to manage it for them.

※ ※ ※

11. ILLUSTRATED LONDON NEWS (JUNE 12 [OR JULY 17], 1897).
Qtd. in Neuphilologisches Centralblatt *11, no. 9 (September 1897): 285.*

[. . .] You have but to get over the difficulty of believing in the existence of vampires in the London of to-day draining the blood of maidens to find Bram Stoker's "Dracula" thrilling interesting. [. . .]

※ ※ ※

12. THE MANCHESTER GUARDIAN (JUNE 15, 1897): 9.

The writer who attempts in the nineteenth century to rehabilitate the ancient legends of the were-wolf and the vampire has set himself a formidable task. Most of the delightful old superstitions of the past have an unhappy way of appearing limp and sickly in the glare of a later day, and in such a story as *Dracula,* by Bram Stoker (Archibald Constable and Co., pp. 390, 6s.), the reader must reluctantly acknowledge that the region for horrors has shifted its ground. Man is no longer in dread of the monstrous and the unnatural, and although Mr. Stoker has tackled his gruesome subject with enthusiasm, the effect is more often grotesque than terrible. The Transylvanian site of Castle Dracula is skilfully chosen, and the picturesque region is well described. Count Dracula himself has been in his day a mediaeval noble, who, by reason of his "vampire" qualities, is unable to die properly, but from century to century resuscitates his life of the "Un-Dead", as the author terms it, by nightly draughts of blood from the throats of living victims, with the appalling consequence that those once so bitten must become vampires in their turn. The plot is too complicated for reproduction, but it says no little for the author's power that in spite of its absurdities the reader can follow the story with interest to the end. It is, however, an artistic mistake to fill a whole volume with horrors. A touch of the mysterious, the terrible, or the supernatural is infinitely more effective and credible.

❋ ❋ ❋

13. WESTMINSTER GAZETTE [LONDON] (JUNE 15, 1897): 3.

MR. BRAM STOKER'S DRACULA

Whoever desires to sup deep horrors should procure Mr. Bram Stoker's new story *Dracula* (Constable). It is about as fine a collection of blood-curdling incidents as we remember to have seen. The interest centers round the Count whose name the novel bears, who is possessed of the attributes and powers of a vampire. At the very outset we are transported to Transylvania, which is, so to speak, the ancestral land of the vampire superstition, and see "Dracula" at home in a lonely castle among the mountains—if spectral beings of "Dracula's" kind can be said to have a home. Later, the scene is transferred to England, and it is here that the main portion of the ghastly drama is enacted. *Dracula,* it should be said, is a story of to-day—indeed, the *Westminster Gazette* plays a small part in the plot; and the fact that Mr. Stoker has been able to work out such a conception amid up-to-date surroundings without the reader's credulity being too much strained shows the skill with which he has performed his task. The text takes the form of extracts from private journals, which no doubt lend to the narrative a naturalness it would not otherwise possess,[12] although once or twice readers may wonder how the characters can sit down to write up their diaries in the extraordinary circumstances in which they find themselves placed. *Dracula* cannot be called a pleasant tale—there is too much of the weird and ghoulish about it for that; but it shows considerable imaginative power, and is possibly the most successful, as it is certain the most ambitious, of Mr. Stoker's efforts.

✳ ✳ ✳

14. THE STAGE
[LONDON] (JUNE 17, 1897).

DRACULA

Mr. Bram Stoker has already made his mark as a writer of romances, but in his latest book, *Dracula*, just published by Archibald Constable & Co., he has done more ambitious work. Grim legends in which strange beings such as Were-Wolf and Vampire are represented as preying upon human life have for ages found a place in European folklore, and a theme of this weird and eerie kind Mr. Bram Stoker has worked out with the zeal and ingenuity of a Wilkie Collins, telling his story, we should add, entirely by means of letters, diaries and memoranda written by various personages, and afterwards typewritten, with all the sets of facts arranged in chronological order. In surrounding his gruesome and fantastically supernatural root idea with a framework plainly matter-of-fact and purely of 19th Century structure, Mr. Stoker has, we think, gone too far in the introduction of complicated details. As the book also contains much about hypnotism medically employed, semi-medieval philosophy, and applications of the latest information concerning the workings of the abnormal brain, it must be conned very carefully indeed if the reader wishes to grasp all the threads in the author's elaborately constructed argument. The opening chapters of Mr. Stoker's brilliant tour de force describing, almost as it were by way of prologue, the first journey of the young English solicitor to the lonely Transylvanian castle haunted by the lonely Vampire or Un Dead, Count Dracula, and his three ghostly sisters who share his avidity for sucking human blood, give the reader at once the proper "atmosphere," and this section of the book has been more artistically done than the somewhat involved and disjointed conclusion that deals with the pursuit of the dreadful Count and his capture and mercilessly merciful true death[13] just as he is regaining his ancestral lair. Mr. Stoker has a keen eye for the picturesque and the appropriate in his choice of epithets and in his word-painting, and many passages of his story are indeed remarkably written. Those who know the Rev. S. Baring Gould's little volume on the Were-Wolf, a theme also touched on here and there by Kipling, may possibly not be repelled by the grisly details of two beautiful and virtuous women having the veins in their throats sucked by the red lips, and lacerated by the gleaming white teeth of this centuries-old Transylvanian warrior and statesman, who often appears as a gaunt wolf and a huge bat. Still more horrible is the scene where the solicitor's brave wife is actually forced by the Vampire to quaff his own nauseating blood, and Mr. Stoker's treatment of the semi-spiritual connection, even at a great distance, thus established between the Count and his second English victim, recalls one of Bulwer Lytton's novels.

A careful study of the zoophagous maniac who after devouring flies and spiders, is tempted by the Count to taste human blood is one of the most interesting things in a volume full of excellently drawn character sketches; the old Amsterdam Professor, for instance, with his curious blend of ancient and modern science and Catholic superstitions, the self-sacrificing young American, and the asylum doctor, being admirably depicted. A white mist, sea-fog, specks of dust floating in the air, are among the elemental machinery employed by Mr. Stoker, who also lays stress upon the development of canine teeth in Dracula's prey, and brings in, mutatis mutandis, the stabbing of women recently notorious in London.[14] The author has, perhaps, knocked the nail too often upon the head in his constant allusions to the exact periods of the day during which the Un Dead may arise from their mouldy earth-filled coffins, but yet all who are attracted by the supernatural in literature will find fascination enough in Mr Stoker's *Dracula*. We must not omit to mention that one of the most effective elements of horror rests in the fact that the Vampire's victims, unless purified by a terrible process we need not describe, become, even after their natural death, of the corruption-spreading family of the Un Dead.

* * *

15. THE LIVERPOOL DAILY POST (JUNE 17, 1897): 4-5.

MR. BRAM STOKER has achieved a feat in fiction. He has written a story scarcely a line of which is credible, but every line of which tends to compel belief. It is a tale of a Vampire—indeed of Vampires, and of Vampirism brought into modern life. So long and intricate a concatenation of loathsome horrors has not before been attempted, but this author has known how to sweeten the fetid path and to light the gloomy windings of the Vampire legend with much loving and happy human nature, much heroism, much faithfulness, much dauntless hope, so that as one phantasmal ghastliness follows another in horrid swift succession the reader is always accompanied by images of devotion and friendliness. There have doubtless been many previous Vampire fictions. There have certainly been several Vampire melodramas. The last was called "The Vampire," and was produced by Charles Kean at the Princess's Theatre about 1852 or 1853. Mr. Boucicault, the author of it, playing in it, but not in his own name, and convicting the Vampire of a very unlikely Irish origin by exclaiming "Lay me out in the moon-bames." There can scarcely have ever been a treatment of the Vampire theme so exhaustive in its draught on literature and lore and at the same time so real and lifelike in its bold adaptation of old-world theories to modern conditions as Mr. Stoker's "Dracula."

Dracula is the name of a Transylvanian Count. He occupies a castle in a lofty, romantic, and almost inaccessible situation, and Mr. Bram Stoker begins his tale with a description of his hero's approach to this eerie seat which illustrates his power of weird description. The incident has much of the effect of Browning's Roland's approach to the dark tower, *plus* a number of strange and alarming incidents which are felt at once to be uncanny, and which eventually prove to be associated with the supernatural element and essence of the narrative. This is only one of many instances of the scenic power of Mr. Bram Stoker's pen, which becomes picturesque whenever there is a suitable opportunity, and indeed supplies appropriate colouring and shading for every phase of description. We cannot give any adequate idea of the difficulties the inventor of this noisome fiction has had to surmount without revealing too many of the incidents, but these, while freshly and most vividly told, are consonant with the traditions of the subject, in which Mr. Stoker's imagination revels with extraordinary energy. What is most admirable in his work is the power with which he compels the acceptance of the things which he recites and the skill with which he gives his riveted readers pure sweet air of wholesome human nature to breathe while conducting them through an ever-deepening, ever increasingly abominable swamp of pestilential miasma.

In accomplishing this he introduces us to some very interesting and pleasant people. One of these is herself a victim of the Vampire fiend, and some of the most extraordinary peculiarities of Vampirism are enacted in herself. The horror of this is all the more poignant because of the charm of her character, and as she has recently refused two suitors and accepted one, the novelist, with equal ingenuity and probability, has planned his plot upon the basis of the co-operation of these three men in the tremendous undertaking of destroying the Vampiric Count by the only method to which Vampires yield. They have the aid of a Dutch professor, whose vigour, science, resource, humour, and sententiousness afford fresh and virile interest, and also the assistance of a remarkable young pair—a solicitor and his wife. All these are banded together in the most remarkable manner by the author. All are excellent, wholesome, agreeable people. All are systematic workers. Most of them keep diaries, and write out notes. Their struggle with the Vampire and his miscellaneous weird coadjutors are carried on from day to day, night to night, hour to hour, with the utmost particularity of detail, the reader of the story knowing from moment to moment as much as those who are actors in it. To give a clear idea of how this is done and what it amounts to would be easy, but would not be fair to the story-teller. Everyone can understand that to read such a story at all one must for the time accept the author's conditions. We must for the time assume the possibility of Vampire life extending by what seems miracle over centuries of diabolical life, always mingling with and at first seeming to be of the ordinary life of the time. We must be content to learn more and more of the ways of the Vampires, of the multiplication of Vampires, of their terrible arts, of their peculiar corruption, of their baneful contamination, of their various disguises, of the charms that tell against them, of the awful means by which during life and after death escape from Vampire conditions may be made, of the indescribable awfulness of the state of anyone upon whom a Vampire has fastened. All this must be accepted for reading and imaginative purposes just as we accept the witches in "Macbeth," their hell-broth, their "deed without a name"—just as we accept Caliban writhing in the aches and pains of Prospero's magic—just as we accept the monster of Frankenstein—just as we accept the roamings through the ages of the Wandering Jew[15]—just as in a lighter vein We accept the travels of Gulliver in Lilliput and the natural history of the Houyhnhnms.

By the canon of literary appreciation which is applied in such cases two things are required. The author of any such work has to produce a web of invention which is interesting and it must hold consistently together. By both of these tests Mr. Bram Stoker will be proved to have added greatly to his evidences of power as a writer of fiction, and those evidences are especially strong and interesting because not only has he kept the Vampire part of his story consistent with itself, but he has dovetailed it consistently with the simple human proceedings of the non-Vampire *dramatis personae*, and these again act at all points consistently with their characters and consistently with the circumstances which the extraordinary Vampire element brings them into. There is indeed another question which we shall not attempt to decide. There will be those who will say that the ghastly and sanguinary details of this fiction are too gross and terrible to be tolerated. The only answer is that they had to be plainly indicated if the story was to be told at all, and that Mr. Bram Stoker has depicted them with searching power. Then some will say, why need the story have been told at all? That will be best answered by the readiness of the public to read it. A theme which has in so many ages engaged the imagination of the world may well tempt a new writer so capable of dealing with it. And though no one will dogmatically accept the Vampire facts there may be utility in the suggestion of the enormous struggle which in some form or another must always be going on between man and unknown forces surrounding him; and there is deep moral interest even under tragically improbable conditions in the spectacle of loyal human beings pursuing a heroic path of effort, howsoever encompassed and howsoever defeated again and again by the powers of evil. We will not pay the author of "Dracula" the banal compliment often paid to Ibsen by the less wise of his admirers: we will not read mystical meaning into the incidents of his story. He probably desired only to make a telling and at the same time human story of the ghastly Vampire legend. But when a man of thought and sensibility works up a superstition for literary purposes in a human manner he is sure to touch deeper sympathies. A thoughtful person may be repaid for reading "Dracula," not only by its engrossing interest, not only by the pathos of its natural side, but by the impression it produces of the limitations by accident and by physical and moral exigency which environ the best and most arduous exertions of the best and most assiduous men and women. There is no interdiction of human endeavour in this. On the contrary, the heavy odds—as, for instance, in the struggle against intemperance where the drink disease has a hold—should rather stimulate to more intense strivings. But the truth remains that the struggle of the good people in Mr. Bram Stoker's story with the foul supernatural craft and force fictitiously attributed to the Vampires is not more herculean than the contest that has to be waged in real life against many forms of seemingly invincible evil.

    The Rev. Thomas Mozley, the celebrated leading-article writer of the *Times*, says in his memoirs:— "There is no public property so universal, so vast, so fertile, so unfailing, as that region of fancy in which the mind creates or accepts creations. What they profess to be signifies little. They may have gained admittance as possible verities, or as plausible fictions; they may have claimed to instruct or to amuse; they may have demanded entrance or insinuated themselves. Once in, they hold their ground and become part of our existence. One thing they are not. They are not matter of-fact, reasonable creatures. They are above human nature, or below it, or beside it altogether. They are incarnations. They occupy the mind and monopolise it. We may say that they are inventions, and that they are indeed nothing at all; but they possess us, influence us, master us, and are our lords. The historian is always hampered with the difficulties of circumstance, the conflict of authorities, and the obligations of truth. The novelist, the poet, or the dramatist sours over mundane obstacles. He creates personages, principalities, and power, in the air. We cannot know everything, or more than a very little. What we do know we cannot know rightly. We must see fact itself through a medium of fiction. But of pure fiction itself we can all take in considerable quantity, a whole world of it indeed." And, as we have just suggested, there may come even of the wildest fiction something more than a mere amusement or excitement.

※ ※ ※

16. COUNTRY LIFE ILLUSTRATED [LONDON] 1 (JUNE 19, 1897): 676.

BOOKS OF THE DAY

"The thing in the coffin writhed, and a hideous, blood-curling screech came from the opened red lips. The body shook and quivered and twisted in wild contortions; the sharp white teeth champed together till the lips were cut, and the mouth was smeared with a crimson foam. But Arthur never faltered. He looked like a figure of Thor as his untrembling arm rose and fell, driving deeper and deeper the mercy-bearing stake, whist the blood from the pierced heart welled and spurted up round." This passage is quoted not from any work of that past-master or horri-

DRACULA. 6s.
By BRAM STOKER.

"One of the most enthralling and unique romances ever written."—*The Christian World.*

"The very weirdest of weird tales."—*Punch.*

"Its fascination is so great that it is impossible to lay it aside."—*The Lady.*

"The idea is so novel that one gasps, as it were, at its originality."—*St. Paul's.*

"While it will thrill the reader, it will fascinate him too much to put it down till he has finished it."—*Bristol Mercury.*

"It is just one of those books which will inevitably be widely read and talked about."—*Lincoln Mercury.*

"A preternatural story of singular power."—*Dublin Freeman's Journal.*

"The characters are limned in a striking manner."—*Manchester Courier.*

"Arrests and holds the attention by virtue of new ideas."—*Shrewsbury Chronicle.*

"Fascinates the imagination and keeps the reader chained."—*Western Times.*

"The most original work of fiction in this almost barren season."—*Black and White.*

"We read it with a fascination which was irresistible."—*Birmingham Gazette.*

"The spell of the book, while one is reading it, simply perfect."—*Woman.*

"The sensation of the season." — *Weekly Liverpool Courier.*

"The reader hurries on breathless from the first page to the last, afraid to miss a single word."—*Daily Telegraph.*

Press notices for Dracula from 1897.

ble description, Edgar Allan Poe, but a story coming under the title, "Dracula," from the pen of Mr. Bram Stoker and from the house of Constable. The extract serves a double purpose. It shows, in the first place, that Mr. Stoker has at command such lurid power as no man has wielded since the scapegrace American genius died, and to men and women who have no desire for blood-curdling literature it may serve as a useful warning. Vampires, of the human variety, are the subject of the book, the most unnatural natural history of them is investigated, and the semi-scientific and semi-superstitious methods by which they may be destroyed are indicated with a ghastly skill that compels admiration. Space will hardly permit us to give an outline of the plot, but it is worth while to pick out a few salient features and characteristics of the vampire, so that our readers may know how to deal with it if they happen to come across one. The vampire, or "Undead," is an inhuman human beast which preys in the night season and is powerless by day. At night it has the strength of twenty men, and is invulnerable to ordinary weapons; but crucifixes, sacred wafers, and, oddly enough, garlic, are potent charms against it. For this reason, since all Spain reeks with garlic, there are, presumably, no vampires in Spain. Vampirism is contagious. The victims of the vampire become vampires themselves after death. Even before death their canine teeth become sharp and elongated, and after death the most charming young women, having been infected with the vampire poison in life, take to flitting about and gorging themselves upon the blood of children at Hampstead Heath. The life of the vampire's victim may be prolonged for a time by transfusion of blood; but this process has its drawbacks, because the longer the vampire's victim is kept alive the more pestilent does the victim become in the dead undead state of vampirism. In fact, vampirism is like hydrophobia, but worse, and the short way of dealing with vampires is to destroy them. How that is done our opening extract shows in part, but the gruesome process is not accomplished until the head has been severed from the body and the mouth has been stuffed full of garlic. A shorter and more certain cure seems not to have occurred to the eminent men of science who figure in Mr. Stoker's pages. The vampire depends for his "peskiness" simply on his canines. Why not call in a dentist to play the part of the God from the Car? He could sterilise the fiercest vampire. But if the learned German Van Helsings *[sic]* had seen this obvious cure Mr. Stoker could not have written a grim, weird, and fascinating story, and that would have been a thousand pities.

* * *

17. THE ATHENAEUM [LONDON], NO. 3635 (JUNE 26, 1897): 835.

Stories and novels appear just now in plenty stamped with a more or less genuine air of belief in the visibility of supernatural agency. The strengthening of a bygone faith in the fantastic and magical view of things in lieu of the purely material is a feature of the hour, a reaction—artificial, perhaps, rather than natural—against late tendencies in thought. Mr. Stoker is the purveyor of so many strange wares that 'Dracula' reads like a determined effort to go, as it were, "one better" than others in the same field. How far the author is himself a believer in the phenomena described is not for the reviewer to say. He can but attempt to gauge how far the general faith and witches, warlocks, and vampires—supposing it to exist in any general and appreciable measure—is likely to be stimulated by this story. The vampire idea is very ancient indeed, and there are in nature, no doubt, mysterious powers to account for the vague belief in such beings. Mr. Stoker's way of presenting his matter, and still more the matter itself, are of too direct and uncompromising a kind. They lack the essential note of awful remoteness and at the same time subtle affinity that separates while it links our humanity with unknown beings and possibilities hovering on the confines of the known world. 'Dracula' is highly sensational, but it is wanting in the constructive art as well as in the higher literary sense it reads at times like a mere series of grotesquely incredible events; but there are better moments that show more power, though even these are never productive of the tremor such subjects evoke under the hand of a master. An immense amount of energy, a certain degree of imaginative faculty, and many ingenious and gruesome details are there. At times Mr. Stoker almost succeeds in creating a sense of possibility in impossibility; at others he merely commands an array of crude statements of incredible actions. The early part goes best, for it promises to unfold the roots of mystery and fear lying deep in human nature; but the want of skill and fancy grows more and more conspicuous. The people who banned themselves together to run the vampire to earth have no real individuality or being. The German *[sic]* man of science is particularly poor, and indulges, like a German in much weak sentiment. Still Mr. Stoker has got together a number of "horrid details," and his object, assuming it to be ghastliness, is fairly well fulfilled. Isolated scenes and touches are probably quite uncanny enough to please those for whom they are designed.

✱ ✱ ✱

18. PUNCH, OR THE LONDON CHARIVARI NO. 112 (JUNE 26, 1897): 327.

OUR BOOKING-OFFICE

"I wants to make your flesh creep," might Mr. Bram Stoker well say as a preface to his latest book, named *Dracula,* which he has given in charge of the Constables (& Co.) to publish. The story is told in diaries and journals, a rather tantalising and somewhat wearisome form of narration, whereof WILKIE COLLINS was a pastmaster. In almost all ghostly, as in most detective stories, one character must never be absent from the *dramatis personae,* and that is The Inquiring, Sceptical, Credulous Noodle. The

REVIEWS & REACTIONS   57

Inquiring Noodle of Fiction must be what in comedy "CHARLES his friend" is to the principal comedian, "only more so", as representing the devoted, admiring slave of the philosophic astute hero, ever ready to question, ever ready to dispute, ever ready to make a mistake at the critical moment, or to go to sleep just when success depends on his remaining awake. "Friend JOHN" is Mr. BRAM STOKER's Noodle-in-Chief. There are also some secondary Noodles; Noodles of no importance. This weird tale is about Vampires, not a single quiet creeping Vampire, but a whole brood of them, governed by a Vampire Monarch, who is apparently a sort of first cousin to *Mephistopheles*. Rats, bats, wolves and vermin obey him, but his power, like that of a certain well-advertised soap, "which will *not* wash clothes," has its limits; and so at last he is trapped, and this particular brood of vampires is destroyed as utterly as would be a hornets' nest when soused with hot pitch. It is a pity that Mr. BRAM STOKER was not content to employ such supernatural anti-vampire receipts as his wildest imagination might have invented without rashly venturing on a domain where angels fear to tread. But for this, the Baron could have unreservedly recommended so ingenious a romance to all who enjoy the very weirdest of weird tales.
—*The Baron de B.-W. [or "Book-Worms"]*

※ ※ ※

19. VANITY FAIR: A WEEKLY SHOW OF POLITICAL, SOCIAL AND LITERARY WARES [LONDON] (JUNE 29, 1897): 80.

BOOKS TO READ, AND OTHERS

Dracula. By Bram Stoker. Constable. This being a year of records, Mr. Bram Stoker appears to have set himself to beat one, and to some extent he has succeeded admirably. His task has been that of outvieing all predecessors in the race for writing the ghastliest books imaginable; and having fixed upon the ghastliest and quite the nastiest subject—a Human Vampire—he has written that vampire up for all he is worth. A most incredible set these vampires of Mr. Bram Stoker's, against whom so much human wit and energy is so fruitlessly pitted, but upon whom a sprig of garlic has the same effect as an open drain on a more ordinary person. Vampires simply can't stand garlic, Mr. Stoker tells us—a useful hint—and if you combine garlic with a stake of wood you have the vampire quite *hors de combat*. We did not know how sensitive these blood-loving people were, but it is well to be prepared.

Speaking quite seriously, this book is really very praiseworthy, and we have not the slightest doubt that it will have the desirable effect of sending some Girton young lady to bed with "the shivers". We became quite absorbed by it, and it is written so well that it is never dull, though it may be sometimes unintentionally funny. But we do not recommend it save to the strong; though perhaps taken with small doses of garlic it may be quite innocuous, even to the weakest.

The cover of Mr. Bram Stoker's book is, like his subject, most forbidding. Indeed, it is the most bilious, vampirous cover we ever remember to have seen. But there is a world of warning in it.

✳ ✳ ✳

20. ST. JAMES' GAZETTE [LONDON] (JUNE 30, 1897).

THE TRAIL OF THE VAMPIRE

There is no more fascinating theme for weird and mysterious fiction than that of the vampire or the were-wolf; and many admirable stories, among which the late Mr. Sheridan Le Fanu's "Carmilla" will always remain conspicuous, have been contrived about these mythical "creatures of the night." We doubt, however, whether any novelist has hitherto worked the mine so thoroughly as has Mr. Bram Stoker in this remarkable new story of his—"Dracula." Certainly we can recall no tale among those of recent date in which the possibilities of horror are more ingeniously drawn out. In the short story, of course, Mr. H. G. Wells can give Mr. Stoker points; but when we remember that "Dracula" fills some four hundred closely printed pages, through which horror follows horror with every wealth of accumulation, we have to confess that its author may fairly boast an achievement of a unique character. There are a hundred nightmares in "Dracula," and each is more uncanny than the last. Moreover, Mr. Stoker is fortunate in the skill with which he makes his imaginative impossibilities appear not only possible but convincing. In securing this end he has followed the method of Wilkie Collins, couching his tale in the form of diary and letter, and adding evidence to evidence with every circumstance of invoice, telegram, and legal document. The fact that this obliges him to represent his characters as writing their journals in the very moment of high emotional pressure may seem to the hypercritical to tax the reader's credulity too far; but, for ourselves, we are disposed to regard this little licence as abundantly justified by its results. Of the plot we have no intention of speaking in detail. Suffice it to say that a young lawyer's clerk is sent on a business errand to one Count Dracula in Transylvania, and that this Count is himself a prince among vampires. After experiencing the most hideous adventures, the young man escapes; but his tormentor follows him to England, tracks him out, and works the death of an innocent and beautiful girl, whose spirit, by the law of the mystery, becomes a vampire in its turn, and is only laid by the intrepid courage of a very interesting German *[sic]* scientist. Gradually the circle of the vampire's influence is widened, and such homely spots as Whitby, Hampstead Heath, and Piccadilly become the scenes of midnight mysteries. Towards the close of the story, where the action quickens and strengthens in intensity, the narrative is remarkably exciting. Altogether "Dracula" is quite the best book Mr. Stoker has yet written, and does great credit alike to his imagination and to his descriptive power.

21. BELGRAVIA: A LONDON MAGAZINE (JULY 1897): 364.

BOOKS OF THE MONTH

Among the younger tale-tellers are Mr. Bram Stoker, with his weird and impressive "Dracula," which will not let one sleep o' nights. —*Davenport Adams*

***

22. THE BRITISH WEEKLY [LONDON] (JULY 1, 1897): 185.

MR. BRAM STOKER.
A CHAT WITH THE AUTHOR OF *DRACULA*

One of the most interesting and exciting of recent novels is Mr. Bram Stoker's "Dracula." It deals with the ancient mediaeval vampire legend, and in no English work of fiction has this legend been so brilliantly treated. The scene is laid partly in Transylvania and partly in England. The first fifty-four pages, which give the journal of Jonathan Harker after leaving Vienna until he makes up his mind to escape from Castle Dracula, are in their weird power altogether unrivalled in recent fiction. The only book which to my knowledge at all compares with them is "The Waters of Hercules," by E.D. Gerard, which also treats of a wild and little known portion of Eastern Europe. Without revealing the plot of the story, I may say that Jonathan Harker, whose diary first introduces the vampire Count, is a young solicitor sent by his employer to Castle Dracula to arrange for the purchase of a house and estate in England.

From the first day of his starting, signs and wonders follow him. At the "Golden Krone" at Bistritz the landlady warns him not to go to Castle Dracula, and, finding that his purpose is unalterable, places a rosary with a crucifix round his neck. For this gift he has good cause to be grateful afterwards. Harker's fellow-passengers on the stage-coach grow more and more alarmed about his safety as they come nearer to the dominions of the Count. Kindly gifts are pressed upon him: wild rose, garlic, and mountain ash. These are meant to be a protection against the evil eye. The author seems to know every corner of Transylvania and all its superstitions. Presently in the Borgo Pass a carriage with four horses drives up beside the coach. "The horses were driven by a tall man with a long brown beard, and a great black hat which seemed to hide his face from us. I could only see the gleam of a pair of very bright eyes, which seemed red in the lamplight as he turned to us.... As he spoke he smiled, and the lamplight fell on a hard-looking mouth, with very red lips and sharp-looking teeth as white as ivory. One of my companions whispered the line from Burger's 'Lenore': 'Denn die Todten reiten schnell' ('For the dead travel fast')."

This is the famous king vampire, Count Dracula, in ancient times a warlike Transylvanian noble. Jonathan Harker is conscious from the first that he is among ghostly and terrible surroundings. Even on the night journey to the Castle, wolves which have gathered round the carriage disappear when the terrible driver lifts his hand. On his arrival the guest is left waiting, and presently a tall old man, whom he suspects from the beginning to be none other than the driver himself, bids him welcome to his house. The Count never eats with his guest. During the day he is absent, but during the night he converses, the dawn breaking up the interview. There are no mirrors to be seen in any part of the ancient building, and the young solicitor's fears are confirmed by the fact that one morning, when the Count comes unexpectedly to his bedroom and stands looking over his shoulder, there is no reflection of him in the small shaving glass Harker has brought from London, and which covers the whole room behind. The adventures of Jonathan Harker will be read again and again; the most powerful part of the book after this is the description of the voyage of the Demeter from Varna to Whitby. A supernatural terror haunts the crew from the moment that they leave the Dardanelles, and as time goes on one man after another disappears. It is whispered that at night a man, tall, thin, and ghastly pale, is seen moving about the ship. The mate, a Roumanian, who probably knows the vampire legend, searches during the day in a number of old boxes, and in one he finds Count Dracula asleep. His own suicide and the death of the captain follow, and when the ship arrives at Whitby, the vampire escapes in the form of a huge dog. The strange thing is that, although in some respects this is a gruesome book, it leaves on the mind an entirely wholesome impression. The events which happen are so far removed from ordinary experience that they do not haunt the imagination unpleasantly. It is certain that no other writer of our day could have produced so marvellous a book.

On Monday morning I had the pleasure of a short conversation with Mr. Bram Stoker, who, as most people know, is Sir Henry Irving's manager at the Lyceum Theatre. He told me, in reply to a question, that the plot of the story had been a long time in his mind, and that he spent about three years in writing it. He had always been interested in the vampire legend. "It is undoubtedly," he remarked, "a very fascinating theme, since it touches both on mystery and fact. In the Middle Ages the terror of the vampire depopulated whole villages."

"*Is there any historical basis for the legend?*"[16]

"It rested, I imagine, on some such case as this. A person may have fallen into a death-like trance and been buried before the time. Afterwards the body may have been dug up and found alive, and from this a horror seized upon the people, and in their ignorance they imagined that a vampire was about. The more hysterical, through excess of fear, might themselves fall into trances in the same way; and so the story grew that one vampire might enslave many others and make them like himself. Even in the single villages it was believed that there might be many such creatures. When once the panic seized the population, their only thought was to escape."

"*In what parts of Europe has this belief been most prevalent?*"

"In certain parts of Styria[17] it has survived longest and with most intensity, but the legend is common to many countries, to China, Iceland, Germany, Saxony, Turkey, the Chersonese, Russia, Poland, Italy, France, and England, besides all the Tartar communities."

"*In order to understand the legend, I suppose it would be necessary to consult many authorities?*"

Mr. Stoker told me that the knowledge of vampire superstitions shown in "Dracula" was gathered from a great deal of miscellaneous reading.[18]

"No one book that I know of will give you all the facts. I learned a good deal from E. Gerard's 'Essays on Roumanian Superstitions,' which first appeared in The Nineteenth Century, and were afterwards published in a couple of volumes. I also learned something from Mr. Baring-Gould's 'Were-Wolves.' Mr. Gould has promised a book on vampires, but I do not know whether he has made any progress with it."

Readers of "Dracula" will remember that the most famous character in it is Dr. Van Helsing, the Dutch physician, who, by extraordinary skill, self-devotion, and labour, finally outwits and destroys the vampire. Mr. Stoker told me that van Helsing is founded on a real character. In a recent leader on "Dracula," published in a provincial newspaper, it is suggested that high moral lessons might be gathered from the book. I asked Mr. Stoker whether he had written with a purpose, but on this point he would give no definite answer, "I suppose that every book of the kind must contain some lesson," he remarked; "but I prefer that readers should find it out for themselves."

In reply to further questions, Mr. Stoker said that he was born in Dublin, and that his work had laid for thirteen years in the Civil Service. He is an M.A. of Trinity College, Dublin. His brother-in-law is Mr. Frankfort Moore, one of the most popular young writers of the day. He began his literary work early. The first thing he published was a book on "The Duties of Clerks of Petty Sessions." Next came a series of children's stories, "Under the

Sunset," published by Sampson Low. Then followed the book by which he has hitherto been best known, "The Snake's Pass." Messrs. Constable have published in their "Acme" library a fascinating little volume called "The Watter's Mou," and this with "The Shoulder of Shasta," completes Mr. Stoker's list of novels. He has been in London for some nineteen years, and believes that London is the best possible place for a literary man. "A writer will find a chance here if he is good for anything; and recognition is only a matter of time." Mr. Stoker speaks of the generosity shown by literary men to one another in a tone which shows that he, at least, is not disposed to quarrel with the critics.

Mr. Stoker does not find it necessary to publish through a literary agent. It always seems to him, he says, that an author with an ordinary business capacity can do better for himself than through any agent. "Some men now-a-days are making ten thousand a year by their novels, and it seems hardly fair that they should pay ten or five percent of this great sum to a middleman. By a dozen letters or so in the course of the year they could settle all their literary business on their own account." Though Mr. Stoker did not say so, I am inclined to think that the literary agent is to him a nineteenth century vampire.

No interview during this week would be complete without a reference to the Jubilee, so I asked Mr. Stoker, as a Londoner of nearly twenty years standing, what he thought of the celebrations. "Everyone," he said, "has been proud that the great day went off so successfully. We have had a magnificent survey of the Empire, and last week's procession brought home, as nothing else could have done, the sense of the immense variety of the Queen's dominions." —*Jane ("Lorna") Stoddard*

* * *

23. SATURDAY REVIEW OF POLITICS, LITERATURE, SCIENCE AND ART [LONDON] 84, NO. 2175 (JULY 3, 1897): 21.

"Dracula." By Bram Stoker. London: Constable. 1897. We had thought that vampires were extinct, but Mr. Bram Stoker has set himself to prove to us the contrary. Or rather he has recreated them with considerable ingenuity and a distinct gift for story-writing of the blood-curdling order. Count Dracula is a vampire of the most exalted kind, for he has lived his life in death for many centuries in his castle in the Carpathians. But Mr. Bram Stoker was not content with the small honour he could have gained by leaving him in an out-of-the-way corner of Europe. That would have been merely to revert to the Mrs. Radcliffe style of fiction. So Count Dracula is brought to London, and Jonathan Harker, a quite ordinary everyday solicitor, has a very bad time with him indeed, both in the Carpathians and in England. The vampire Count is hunted down with all the paraphernalia of modern science, combined with the charms and exorcisms of an earlier age, and there is a tremendously exciting pursuit before he is finally cornered. Then his throat is cut, his heart pierced, and his body crumbles into dust. We ourselves confess to a sigh of relief when we knew that so dangerous and literally blood-thirsty a person had ceased to exist, and that Mina Harker was no longer in danger of becoming a vampire like her friend Lucy. Mr. Bram Stoker cannot boast of any elegance of style, but at least he is plain and straightforward, and tells his story without any vulgar claptrap and magniloquent balderdash with which some writers of this class of fiction disfigure their books. Moreover he has been at the pains to get up very carefully all that can be gathered of vampire lore, and has made his book a complete treatise on the habits and customs of these strange beasts. There are many readers who like to sup full of horrors and to feel their flesh creep, and "Dracula" is undoubtedly the book for their money. Nervous persons, young children and sufferers from delirium tremens, will do well not to look within its covers.

66   REVIEWS & REACTIONS

* * *

24. NATIONAL OBSERVER, AND BRITISH REVIEW OF POLITICS, ECONOMICS, LITERATURE, SCIENCE, AND ART [LONDON] 18, NO. 450 (JULY 3, 1897): 334.

DRACULA. BY BRAM STOKER. LONDON: A. CONSTABLE & CO.

With an almost convincing realism, Mr. Stoker has chosen to depict one of the most gruesome creations with which man's morbid imagination has peopled the universe. In working out his subject he has not spared us a single revolting detail; so horrible, in fact, are some of the incidents narrated as to inspire one with the nausea that one feels in lighting suddenly upon vivid descriptions of such terrible events as the recent calamity in Paris. More awful even than the ghoul of the *Arabian Nights* is the Slavonic superstition of the human vampire, which, dead to all intent and purposes during the day, is supposed to prowl around by night and gorge itself with the blood of living man. Out of this fearful legend, which flourished in Eastern Europe a

Left: Press notices for Dracula *from* The Publishers' Circular *and* Booksellers' Record of British and Foreign Literature *67, no. 1621 (July 24, 1897): 73.*

century ago, and still finds credence among the ignorant, Mr. Stoker has spun a romance that will scarcely find its parallel for horror and repulsiveness. The diabolical personality of Count Dracula, who is an archfiend among the vampires, is a blood-curdling conception of appalling monstrosity; and it must have been a terrible ordeal to his English guest to have witnessed him crawling down the castle wall, *face down*, in the moonlight, with his black cloak spreading out around him like great wings; or to have found his bloated corpse before sunset, blood trickling from the corners of his mouth, as he lay "like a filthy leech, exhausted with his repletion." The plot is ingenious, and the more interesting as it is laid chiefly in England at the present day.

※ ※ ※

25. BLACK AND WHITE: A WEEKLY ILLUSTRATED RECORD AND REVIEW [LONDON] 24, NO. 336 (JULY 10, 1897): 52.

Indubitably the most original work of fiction in this almost barren season is BRAM STOKER'S *Dracula* (Constable), a romance crammed full of horrors, wherein the prosaic is so cunningly commingled with the incredible as to give an impression of verity. Mr. STOKER imprisons his hero in a desolate Russian[19] *[sic]* castle whose very atmosphere is impregnated with thirsty vampires. He encompasses his heroines with like creatures till it seems as though neither God nor man had power to aid them. The pursuit of the vampire over the snow by the avengers has somewhat of the weird fascination of Frankenstein. Assuredly *Dracula* is a book to shudder at.

※ ※ ※

26. THE SPECTATOR: A WEEKLY REVIEW OF
POLITICS, LITERATURE, THEOLOGY, AND ART
[LONDON] 79 (JULY 31, 1897): 150-151.

RECENT NOVELS

Mr. Bram Stoker gives us the impression—we may be doing him an injustice—of having deliberately laid himself out in Dracula to eclipse all previous efforts in the domain of the horrible—to "go one better" than Wilkie Collins (whose method of narration he has closely followed), Sheridan Le Fanu, and all the other professors of the flesh-creeping school. Count Dracula, who gives his name to the book, is a Transylvanian noble who purchases an estate in England, and in connection with the transfer of the property Jonathan Harker, a young solicitor, visits him in his ancestral castle. Jonathan Harker has a terrible time of it, for the Count—who is a vampire of immense age, cunning, and experience—keeps him as a prisoner for several weeks, and when the poor young man escapes from the gruesome charnel-house of his host, he nearly dies of brain-fever in a hospital at Buda-Pesth. The scene then shifts to England, where the Count arrives by sea in the shape of a dog-fiend, after destroying the entire crew, and resumes operations in various uncanny manifestations, selecting as his chief victim Miss Lucy Westenra, the fiancée of the Honourable Arthur Holmwood, heir-presumptive to Lord Godalming. The story then resolves itself into the history of the battle between Lucy's protectors, including two rejected suitors—an American and a "mad" doctor—and a wonderfully clever specialist from Amsterdam, against her unearthly persecutor. The clue is furnished by Jonathan Harker, whose betrothed, Mina Murray, is a bosom friend of Lucy's, and the fight is long and protracted. Lucy succumbs, and, worse still, is temporarily converted into a vampire. How she is released from this unpleasant position and restored to a peaceful post-mortem existence, how Mina is next assailed by the Count, how he is driven from England, and finally exterminated by the efforts of the league—for all these, and a great many more thrilling details, we must refer our readers to the pages of Mr. Stoker's clever but cadaverous romance. Its strength lies in the invention of incident, for the sentimental element is decidedly mawkish. Mr. Stoker has shown considerable ability in the use that he has made of all the available traditions of vampirology, but we think his story would have been all the more effective if he had chosen an earlier period. The up-to-dateness of the book-the phonograph diaries, typewriters, and so on—hardly fits in with the medieval methods which ultimately secure the victory for Count Dracula's foes.

* * *

27. THE ACADEMY: A WEEKLY REVIEW OF LITERATURE, SCIENCE, AND ART, NO. 1317 (JULY 31, 1897): 98.

BOOK REVIEWS REVIEWED

"Dracula." By Bram Stoker. (Constable.) Mr. Bram Stoker's book is explained to be a version of the "were-wolf" legend, of which the setting is England of the present day, and the manner in the documentary system of many hands favoured by Wilkie Collins. The translation of the monster to English soil is pronounced by the *Speaker* to be a distinct success; and "it says much for the author's command of his gruesome theme that in spite of being thus handicapped in his methods, he has succeeded in making the story intensely interesting. . . . The supernatural element is managed with . . . an appearance of realism that is extremely ingenious." The *Chronicle* pronounces that "the impossibilities of the subject are handled with such fertility and ingenuity that *Dracula* is not likely to leave room for imitators. Mr. Stoker's vampire will remain unique." The story, says the *Pall Mall*, "is horrid and creeping to the last degree. It is also excellent, and one of the best things in the supernatural line is we have been lucky enough to get on. . . . Mr. Stoker as mastered the real secrets a genuine 'creep'; . . . and there is creep in every dozen pages or so." The *Daily News* asks, what of the general decay of faith? "Here...is him Mr. Bram Stoker taking in hand the old ice and world legend of the were-wolf, or vampire, with all its weird and exciting associations of blood-sucking and human-flesh-devouring, and interweaving it with the threads of a long story with an earnestness, a directness, and a simple good faith which ought to go far to induce readers of fiction to surrender their imagination and the novelist's hands." "Never," writes Mr. Courtney in the *Daily Telegraph*, "what is so mystical a tale told with such simple verisimilitude." But he find something opposed to "moderate ethical principles" in the idea of the innocent persons who, by the extraneous influence of the monster develop a like unnatural lust. "Mr. Bram Stoker," writes the *Saturday*, "cannot boast of any elegance of style; but at least he is plain and straight-forward, and he tells the story without him any of the vulgar clap-trap and magniloquent balderdash with which some writers of this class of fiction disfigure their books."

※ ※ ※

28. THE BOOKMAN: AN ILLUSTRATED LITERARY JOURNAL [NEW YORK] 12, NO. 71 (AUGUST 1897): 129.

DRACULA. By Bram Stoker. 6s. (A. Constable.) Since Wilkie Collins left us we have had no tale of mystery so liberal in matter and so closely woven. But with the intricate plot, and the methods of the narrative, the resemblance to stories of the author of "The Woman in White" ceases; for the audacity and the horror of "Dracula" are Mr. Stoker's own. A summary of the book would shock and disgust; but we must own that, though here and there in the course of the tale we hurried over things with repulsion, we read nearly the whole with rapt attention. It is something of a triumph for the writer that neither the improbability, nor the unnecessary number of hideous incidents recounted of the man-vampire, are long foremost in the reader's mind, but that the interest of the danger, of the complications, of the pursuit of the villain, of human skill and courage pitted against inhuman wrong and superhuman strength, rises always to the top. Keep "Dracula" out of the way of nervous children, certainly; but a grown reader, unless he be of unserviceably delicate stuff, will both shudder and enjoy from p. 35, when Harker sees the Count "emerge from the window and begin to crawl down the castle wall over that dreadful abyss, *face down*, with his cloak spreading out around him like great wings."

※ ※ ※

29. THE OBSERVER [LONDON] (AUGUST 1, 1897).

Those who are wishful for a veritable feast of horrors need seek no farther than the present work, for in it Mr. Stoker has been pleased to weave a romance of vampires and their habits. Not only is the subject gruesome, but the author's undoubted descriptive powers make the various ghastly experiences startlingly realistic, and engender a fascination which forces one to read on to the end. From start to finish the book, though long, is wildly exciting, and the account of the terrible midnight drive in the first chapter is one of a series of fierce struggles against the repulsive Count Dracula, which end only on the last page. The story is set forth in various diaries and letters, a style which is apt to prove somewhat confusing. It speaks well for the author's skill in this case that the plot is plainly traceable throughout. Notwithstanding the merits of the book, it is impossible to congratulate Mr. Stoker on his theme, which can but feel to be one quite unworthy of his literary capabilities.

***

30. DAILY MAIL [LONDON] (AUGUST 6, 1897): 3.

CHAT ABOUT BOOKS

It is clear that holiday-makers prefer, on the whole, the merely entertaining novels rather than the didactic and the instructive. [The reviewer then lists several books by "authors at present most in vogue at the seaside" noting "a large demand." The list includes *Dracula*.]

***

31. PUBLISHERS' CIRCULAR AND BOOKSELLERS' RECORD OF BRITISH AND FOREIGN LITERATURE [LONDON], NO. 1623 (AUGUST 7, 1897): 131.

From Messrs. Archibald Constable & Co.—Dracula, by Bram Stoker. In 'Dracula' Mr. Bram Stoker has given us one of the most weird and gruesome tales of modern times; in fact, after reading it, we might almost term him the Edgar Allan Poe of the nineties.[20] *Dracula* is a story which takes hold of the reader soon after the opening pages. The story is told by way of extracts from diaries kept by various people, the first being the journal kept by Jonathan Harker, solicitor of Exeter, who is on his way to the Carpathians to visit Count Dracula at his castle of Dracula, to complete certain documents connected with the purchase by the Count of a small property near London. Jonathan Harker undergoes some awful experiences in the castle, and finally escapes from it alive, but in a fever, which attacks his brain and keeps him to his bed for many weeks. It turns out that Dracula is a human vampire, and now that Harker has escaped he tries to wreak his vengeance on him, not by attacking him and killing him outright, but by planning a series of tortures on those nearest and dearest to him. The first one attacked is Lucy, friend of Mina Murray. Mina is engaged to Harker and marries him. Lucy dies a vampire, and thereafter leaves her coffin at sundown and returns at dawn. Every night she claims a victim until Harker, aided by a Dutch doctor, Van Helsing, and Dr. Seward of a lunatic asylum near London, and two other men, overcome the wiles of the Count and secure peace for Lucy's body. Mina is the next to fall a victim and is discovered by Van Helsing gloating over her husband who is asleep. She has just begun her feast of blood when the doctor stops her. The struggle against the fiendish Count continues till he is forced to fly from England. The group of heroes, with Mina, pursue him to his dreaded castle in the Carpathians, and here the final blow is struck and the terrible vampire's power is shattered. Mr. Bram Stoker shows remarkable skill in the management of the story, which is the best he has written. It is certainly the cleverest book of the kind we have come across for a long time, and we confess to having sat up to an unconscionable hour of the early morning to finish it.

※ ※ ※

32. THE GUARDIAN [LONDON], NO. 2697 (AUGUST 11, 1897): 1248-1249.

NOVELS

For uncanny gruesomeness it would be hard to find anything to equal the first half or two-thirds of Mr. Bram Stoker's *Dracula*. Possibly the dragging effect of the latter portion is due as much to the reader's imagination being satiated with horrors as to anything else. Nevertheless, horrors lose something of their terrors with familiarity, and to repeat certain gruesome ceremonies in a detailed fashion three times as Mr. Stoker does is not well advised. He has, of course, done so to heighten the realistic effect, but the result is not entirely successful. The story is told in the diaries of the various characters, and a few letters. The first diary is that of Jonathan Harker, and records how he was sent on business by the solicitors' firm of which he was a member to a castle in Transylvania, the property of one Count Dracula. It tells of the horror with which the peasants and travellers whom he met on his journey heard of his destination, of the night drive accompanied by the horrible howling of wolves and their occasional appearance, of his arrival at the castle and partial reassurance from the courtly manners and appearance of his host. Then comes the return of his half-allayed uneasiness, the discovery that he is practically a prisoner in the castle, with the Count as sole companion and gaoler, then the worse discovery of horrors too great for a sane man to believe in—the sight of his host going out like a great bat, and returning with human food for the benefit of creatures more terrible almost than himself. Jonathan's diary closes with his recorded intention to escape or lose his life in the attempt. Then follows the journal of Mina Murray, afterwards Mina Harker, and certain letters exchanged between her and Lucy Westenra. In the journal is pasted an extract from a local paper describing the coming ashore in an awful storm of a ship having on board only a dead man fastened by his hands, between which is a crucifix, to the wheel, and a big dog, which jumps on land and escapes. The dead man has attached to his cloths an account of his voyage, and the mysterious disappearance of his crew. Next comes Dr. Leward's[21] *[sic]* diary, wherein is set down among other matters Lucy Westenra's mysterious illness, the efforts to save her life made by Van Helsing, a rather tiresome Dutch specialist, and her apparent death. More and more ghastly grows the story as Van helsing gradually reveals to the other characters the meaning of Lucy's illness—that she has been bitten by a vampire, worse still that her spirit is now held by a vampire spirit, and induces them to fight with him to free her from unreal death. With Lucy's real death the more impressive scenes seem to us over, though there are plenty more horrible ones in the crusade entered upon by a devoted band against the particular vampire which has started the mischief. It says much for Mr. Bram Stoker's power that only here and there the reader is able at once to shake himself free from belief in the earlier experiences he imparted to him, and is generally forced to accept them for true from the uncanny matter-of-factness with which they are set forth.

✻ ✻ ✻

33. LETTER FROM ARTHUR CONAN DOYLE TO BRAM STOKER (AUGUST 20, 1897).22

My dear Bram Stoker

I am sure that you will not think it an impertinence if I write to tell you how very much I have enjoyed reading *Dracula*. I think it is the very best story of diablerie which I have read for many years. It is really wonderful how with so much exciting interest over so long a book there is never an anticlimax. It holds you from the very start and grows more and more engrossing until it is quite painfully vivid. The old Professor is most excellent and so are the two girls. I congratulate you with all my heart for having written so fine a book.

With all kindest remembrances to Mrs Bram Stoker & yourself

Yours very truly
A Conan Doyle

✻ ✻ ✻

34. THE TIMES
[LONDON] (AUGUST 23, 1897).

RECENT NOVELS

Dracula cannot be described as a domestic novel, nor its annals as those of a quiet life. The circumstances described are from the first peculiar. A young solicitor sent for on business by a client in Transylvania goes through some unusual experiences. He finds himself shut up in a half ruined castle with a host who is only seen at night and three beautiful females who have the misfortune to be vampires. Their intentions, which can hardly be described as honourable, are to suck his blood, in order to sustain their own vitality. Count Dracula (the host) is also a vampire, but has grown tired of his compatriots, however young and beautiful, and has a great desire for what may literally be called fresh blood. He has therefore sent for the solicitor that through his means he may be introduced to London society. Without understanding the Count's views, Mr. Harker has good reason for having suspicions of his client. Wolves come at his command, and also fogs; he is also too clever by half at climbing. There is a splendid prospect from the castle terrace, which Mr. Harker would have enjoyed but for his conviction that he would never leave the place alive:—

> In the soft moonlight the distant hills became melted, and the shadows in the valleys and gorges of velvety blackness. The mere beauty seemed to cheer me; there was peace and comfort in every breath I drew. As I leaned from the window my eye was caught by something moving a storey below me, and somewhat to my left, where I imagined, from the lie of the rooms, that the windows of the Count's own room would look out. The window at which I stood was tall and deep, stone-mullioned, and, though weather-worn, was still complete, but it was evidently many a day since the casement had been there. I

drew back behind the stonework and looked carefully out.

What I saw was the Count's head coming out from the window. I did not see the face, but I knew the man by the neck and the movement of his back and arms. In any case, I could not mistake the hands, which I had had so many opportunities of studying. I was at first interested and somewhat amused, for it is wonderful how small a matter will interest and amuse a man when he is a prisoner. But my very feelings changed to repulsion and terror when I saw the whole man slowly emerge from the window and begin to crawl down the castle wall over that dreadful abyss, face down, with his cloak spreading out around him like great wings.

These scenes and situations, striking as they are, become commonplace compared with Count Dracula's goings on in London. As Falstaff was not only witty himself but the cause of wit in other people, so a vampire, it seems, compels those it has bitten (two little marks on the throat are its token, usually taken by the faculty for the scratches of a brooch) to become after death vampires also. Nothing can keep them away but garlic, which is, perhaps, why that comestible is so popular in certain countries. One may imagine, therefore, how the thing spread in London after the Count's arrival. The only chance of stopping it was to kill the Count before any of his victims died, and this was a difficult job, for, though several centuries old, he was very young and strong, and could become a dog or a bat at pleasure. However, it is undertaken by four resolute and highly-principled persons, and how it is managed forms the subject of the story, of which nobody can complain that it is deficient in dramatic situations. We would not, however, recommend it to nervous persons for evening reading.

***

35. THE NEW YORK DRAMATIC MIRROR (AUGUST 21, 1897): 8.

GAWAIN'S GOSSIP
(*Special correspondence of The Mirror.*)
London, August 7

If you want a cooler this weather let me advise the reading of Bram Stoker's latest story, "Dracula." It is a vampire thing, and makes your blood run cold in every page.

—GAWAIN

***

36. THE BOOKSELLER: A NEWSPAPER OF BRITISH AND FOREIGN LITERATURE 478 (SEPTEMBER 3, 1897): 816.

Dracula. By Bram Stoker. (A. Constable and Co.)— Though Mr. Bram Stoker has not before now ventured on a six-shilling novel, he has given us several delightful short stories, which proved that he possessed in high degree the vivid imagination and the descriptive faculty, which are such essential elements of the novelist's success. In his present more ambitious effort we find these qualities exhibited in a very remarkable degree. A lawyer's clerk, who goes to visit a Transylvanian noble on matters of business, finds that he has entered an enchanted castle, and that his host is a fiend in human shape—indeed, an instance of the vampire of mystic legend. This being, not content with Transylvania, finds his way mysteriously to England, and succeeds in battening on a young lady, the friend of the young lawyer's intended, and she, after a time, succumbs to her fate, and, worse than all, is endowed with the power of rising from the grave and sucking the blood of any young child she may chance to meet. All this is terribly uncanny and horrible; but Mr. Bram Stoker tells his story with such skill that the reader is interested throughout, and cannot put down the book until the end is reached. The story is told in selections from diaries and similar correspondence, much after the fashion of Wilkie Collins; and, indeed, we can hardly give the book greater praise than to say that it might almost have been written by Mr. Collins himself.

* * *

37. THE LIVERPOOL MERCURY (SEPTEMBER 15, 1897): 9.

BOOKS OF THE DAY

Dracula. By Bram Stoker. (Westminster, Archibald Constable and Company. Price 6s.) Mr. Bram Stoker has chosen a terrible subject for his latest book, and he has worked it out with intimate skill to the end. An old Eastern superstition, still having weight in Hungary, forms the lines upon which the story is based. Vampires and their horrible sustenance are treated in all of their subtle and loathsome nature. "Dracula" is the king of their blood-sucking race. He is portrayed with great dramatic force, and his appearances on the scene become as foreboding to the reader as they are to his victims. The theory concerning vampires is that they live by sucking human blood, and that their victims at death become as awful as themselves, and live in a ghostly state, issuing nightly from their graves in quest for their unholy food. The only way to kill the evil spirit, and restore the human soul to bliss, is to drive a stake through the heart of the seemingly dead body. Fearful shrieks are the immediate result, but afterwards an expression of peace pervades the hitherto wolfish features. It may be seen from

Dracula
By BRAM STOKER. *Price Six Shillings.*

"The reader hurries on breathless from the first page to the last, afraid to miss a single word."—*Daily Telegraph.*
"Unquestionably a striking example of imaginative power."—*Morning Post.*
"The most daring venture into the supernatural I have ever come across."—*Truth.*
"One of the best things in the supernatural line that we have been lucky enough to hit upon."—*Pall Mall Gazette.*
"A story of very real power."—*The Speaker;*
"One of the weirdest romances of late years."—*Lloyd's Newspaper.*
"We have never read any work which so powerfully affected the imagination."—*North British Daily Mail.*
"Interesting almost to fascination."—*Gloucester Journal.*
"An exciting story from beginning to end."—*The Newsagent.*
"Told in a way to hold the reader spell-bound."—*Sunderland Weekly Echo.*
"Contains many passages of rare power and beauty."—*Dundee Advertiser.*
"Will remain unique amongst the terrors which paralyse our nerves at bedtime."—*Daily Chronicle.*
"The story is indeed a strange and fascinating one."—*Northern Whig.*
"I soon became horribly enthralled, and could not choose but read on—on—until the lights burned blue and my blood ran cold."—*The Referee.*
"No other writer of the day could have produced so marvellous a book."—*The British Weekly.*
"The new wild and weird 'Vampire' story."—*The Morning.*

Press notices for Dracula *from* Songs of Love and Empire *(Archibald Constable & Co., 1898): 176.*

this brief sketch that there is plenty of room for imaginative writing, and Mr. Stoker makes every possible use of his material. The result is a recital of terrible and bloodcurdling interest, fraught with every possible horror, and absorbingly interesting from beginning to end.

* * *

38. LONDON QUARTERLY REVIEW 29, NO. 1 (OCTOBER 1897): 175.

Dracula, by Ben [sic] Stoker (6s.), is vampire story before which Mr. Baring Gould's *Marjory of Quether* pales into insignificance. It is full of thrilling adventures, and the way in which the little circle of doctors and brave men set out themselves to track and hunt down the vampire, gives the writer full scope for his talent for blood-curdling situations. It is manifestly based on a careful study of the vampire legends, but it is too horrible for enjoyment. The little sketch of Whitby, which comes in the story, is a gem of description, the quiet beauty of which is the more impressive amid the gruesome things that surround it.

* * *

39. THE SOUTH AUSTRALIAN REGISTER [ADELAIDE, SOUTH AUSTRALIA] (NOVEMBER 6, 1897): 6.

REVIEW OF BOOKS
"Dracula," by Bram Stoker; Hutchinson and Co., London, per George Robertson and Co.—This book is positively unique. We confess to not having conscientiously read every page; for, after having perused the passage which will be presently transcribed, sampling the remaining two or three hundred proved equally paralysing.

"Take this stake in your hand, ready to place the point over the heart, and the hammer in your right," said Van Helsing; "then, when we begin our prayer for the dead—I shall read him, I have here the book—strike in God's name, that so all may be well with the Dead we love, and that the Un-Dead pass away."

"Arthur took the hammer and the stake and placed the point over the heart, and as I looked I could see its dent in the white flesh. Then he struck with all his might.—The Thing in the coffin writhed, and a hideous blood-curdling screech came from the opened red lips. The body shook, and quivered, and twisted in wild contortions; the sharp white teeth champed together till the lips were cut and the mouth was smeared with crimson foam. But Arthur never faltered. He looked like a figure of Thor as his untrembling arm rose and fell, driving deeper and deeper and the mercy-bearing stake, whilst the blood from the pierced heart welled and spurted up around it. And then the writing and quivering of the body became less, and the teeth ceased to champ and the face to quiver. Finally it lay still. The terrible task was over."

We should hardly think that one man was equal to the concoction of 400 pages of this kind of thing. Collaboration must have been resorted to; but we repudiate the notion that any of Dr. Cleland's patients could have piled up the horrors as effectively as the writer of this work has done.

※ ※ ※

40. THE ARGUS [MELBOURNE, VICTORIA, AUSTRALIA] (NOVEMBER 6, 1897): 9.

[. . .] But in Mr. Bram Stoker a writer has arisen who intrepidly assumes that mediæval gullibility is in full survival. He appeals to his readers with the most horrid, yet in some respects the most ludicrous, romance of vampiredom to be found in literature. It is a bold attempt to concentrate the fables and superstitions which have existed in Eastern Europe especially for many centuries into a shape sufficiently like reality to cheat the imagination of the nineteenth century. Can the modest reader be induced to bestow a passing belief upon vampires any more than upon sylphs and salamanders? Where most men would answer no, Mr. Stoker says yes, and confidently tries the experiment. It may be argued that he does no more than imitate the hardlihood Sheridan Le Fanu, but that gifted author contented himself with an outline, and never ventured upon the collaboration of detail with which Mr. Stoker surrounds his vampire Count Dracula and the victims upon whom that monster preys in modern England.

There is an extensive literature upon the subject of vampires, which this author must have studied with a minuteness and assiduity just sufficient to wreck his purpose. For if he had not painted into his gruesome portrait all the habits and characteristics supplied by a wealth of tradition, we could have believed in

PRICE SIX SHILLINGS

Dracula

By BRAM STOKER

" One of the most enthralling and unique romances ever written."
—*The Christian World.*
" The very weirdest of weird tales."—*Punch.*
" Its fascination is so great that it is impossible to lay it aside."—*The Lady.*
" It holds us enthralled."—*The Literary World.*
" The idea is so novel that one gasps, as it were, at its originality. A romance far above the ordinary production."—*St. Paul's.*
" Much loving and happy human nature, much heroism, much faithfulness, much dauntless hope, so that as one phantasmal ghastliness follows another in horrid swift succession the reader is always accompanied by images of devotion and friendliness."—*Liverpool Daily Post.*
" A most fascinating narrative."—*Dublin Evening Herald.*
" While it will thrill the reader, it will fascinate him too much to put it down till he has finished it."—*Bristol Mercury.*
" It is just one of those books which will inevitably be widely read and talked about."—*Lincoln Mercury.*
" A preternatural story of singular power. The book is bound to be a success."—*Dublin Freeman's Journal.*
" The characters are limned in a striking manner."—*Manchester Courier.*
" A decidedly able as exceptionally interesting and dramatically told story."
—*Sheffield Telegraph.*
" We strongly recommend all readers of a sensitive nature or weak nerves to abstain from following the diabolic adventures of Count Dracula."—*Sheffield Independent.*
" Arrests and holds the attention by virtue of new ideas, treated in an uncommon style. Throughout the book there is not a dull passage."—*Shrewsbury Chronicle.*
" Singularly entertaining."—*Birmingham Daily Mail.*
" Fascinates the imagination and keeps the reader chained."—*Western Times* (Exeter).
" We commend it to the attention of readers who like their literary fare strong, and at the same time healthy."—*Oban Times.*
" The most original work of fiction in this almost barren season."—*Black and White.*
" We read it with a fascination which was irresistible."—*Birmingham Gazette.*
" The spell of the book, while one is reading it, is simply perfect."—*Woman.*
" The most blood-curdling novel of the paralysed century."—*Gloucester Journal.*
" The sensation of the season."—*Weekly Liverpool Courier.*

ARCHIBALD CONSTABLE & CO
2 WHITEHALL GARDENS WESTMINSTER

Press notices for Dracula *from* By the Roaring Reuss, Idylls and Stories of the Alps *(Archibald Constable & Co., 1898): 187.*

it better. Vampires—the "living dead," whose corpses cannot decay, but who have the power of rising from their graves at night to batten upon the blood of human beings—are the Vroucolakas of the Greeks. They have been treated of by an old German writer, Michael Raufft, in his learned book "De Masticatione Mortuorum in Tumulis," by the Frenchman Calmet, and by many another grave-faced sifter of mediæval superstitions. All agree that these unpleasant nocturnal prowlers, who stalk abroad murdering and blood-sucking, are most common in certain countries, to writ, Silesia. Hungry. Consequently to Hungry—or rather, well to the eastward of Transylvania—Mr. Stoker betakes himself in search of the home of his foul wanderer. He dwells, half man, half brute, in a gloomy castle in the deepest recesses of the Carpathians, surrounded by a bevy of lovely yet loathsome females, blood-suckers like himself. The mistake is that as Mr. Stoker designs to transport his monster to England, there to feast upon the teeming population of the metropolis, he is tempted to introduce Dracula in too strong a light. The more intimately we regard a vampire and take stock in his proceedings, the more disposed we are to forget horror in scepticism. Ancient records of vampiredom avoided this, partly because they were deliciously vague. Raufft tells mainly of swinish munchings in the grave by certain evil-disposed and voracious corpses, which is a violation of social proprieties, but little more. Calmet, in his dissertation on the vampires of Hungary, contents himself with concluding that there are numbers of "revenants" whose bodies the earth rejects, but he refrains from committing himself to the theory that they may be actually caught either entering or leaving their graves. And he takes the highly sensible view that a pretension of the Greek church, to the effect that the earth would not retain corpses which had come under orthodox excommunication, may be accountable for the prevalence of vampiredom in Slavonic countries.

But no difficulties daunt Mr. Bram Stoker. At close quarters we are shown the vampire endowed with all the attributes which the amalgamated superstitions of the ignorant in all ages have woven about him. He is man insomuch that he must pass the daylight hours in his human form reclining upon a heap of foul-smelling earth, loads of which he conveys with him as personal luggage for this necessary purpose. He casts no shadow, gives back no reflection in any mirror; he can come and go through the merest crevice, can materialise out of moonlight mist, can change at sunrise or sunset to bat or wolf, can command certain of the lower brutes, cannot cross running water save at slack or ebb of tide, can transform all upon whose blood he feasts; and so forth. We are gravely invited by our romancist to contemplate a monster of this perplexing sort astir in busy London—to watch him being fought by energetic, intelligent men of modern world with such weapons as garlic flowers, sacred wafer, and crucifixes. No more staggering demand upon what Mr. Gosse terms "temporary credence" could well be made, for Mr. Bram Stoker writes for a community mainly Protestant and for an age in which belief in the efficacy of relics and symbols has almost disappeared. It is true that the author does not lean over-confidently upon these agents. They can but alleviate the danger to be apprehended from the viciousness of a vampire out on business. The radical cure is effected as of old by knife and pointed stake. Mr. Stoker, though he does presume immensely upon the capacity of modern readers to gape and swallow, concludes that their credulity will not stand a severer test than that of their mediæval ancestors. An infallible corrective of vampiredom has always been to cause the suspected grave to be beaten with a hazel twig wielded by a virgin not less than twenty-five years old. Yet in practice the severed head and the stake driven through the heart were ever preferred. When the pinch comes, our latter-day author discards his theory of remedy by exorcism as gracelessly as his predecessors abandoned the hazel twig.

* * *

41. THE SPEAKER: A REVIEW OF POLITICS, LETTERS, SCIENCE, AND THE ARTS [LONDON] 27 (JANUARY 1, 1898): 29.

THE BLOOD OF THE VAMPIRE. BY FLORENCE MARRYAT. LONDON: HUTCHINSON & CO.

Mr. Bram Stoker has much to answer for. Perhaps, however, when he published his remarkable vampire-story, "Dracula," he failed to foresee the inevitable consequences which its appearance would entail upon readers and critics of contemporary fiction, in the shape of a swarm of ill-conceived and ill-executed imitations by inferior writers. Yet those consequences have, alas! followed only too speedily, and those who were genuinely thrilled and absorbingly interested by the weird fascinations of "Dracula," have since been compelled to own themselves frankly bored by the ubiquitous vampire thrust so perseveringly upon their notice by certain minor novelists. And now here is the indefatigable Miss Florence Marryat off upon the well-worn trail, and trying hard to be fashionably "creepy" in the verbose pages of her latest novel, "The Blood of the Vampire"! Is it necessary to add that she has not succeeded in that ambitious attempt? Miss Marryat is an experienced novelist, who, despite very manifest failings of taste and style, has shown herself the possessor of a certain rough energy and vivacity that have generally made her stories readable, at least, if inartistic and exaggerated; but she never has shown, nor does she show in "The Blood of the Vampire," any trace of the special qualities requisite to such a task as she has here undertaken. The book is a mistake, and we cannot pretend to treat it as a successful experiment. [. . .]

※ ※ ※

REVIEWS & REACTIONS

Cover for the first American edition of Dracula *(Doubleday & McClure Co., 1899).*

42. THE ADVERTISER
[ADELAIDE, SOUTH AUSTRALIA]
(JANUARY 22, 1898): 8.

CURRENT LITERATURE
HUTCHINSON & CO'S PUBLICATIONS
The latest additions to Messrs. Hutchinson's Colonial Library include stories grave and gay, sensational and domestic. Pre-eminently striking is Bram Stoker's "Dracula," notwithstanding that it is in great part a reversion to old-fashioned methods. Its plot is unfolded by letters and diaries in regular painstaking fashion, after the manner of Wilkie Collins. As for the plot itself, it is ghastly beyond belief. Not even Sheridan Lefanu in his wildest moments ever conceived anything to equal it for haunting horror. It is a story of human vampires and demoniacal possession, of midnight apparitions and life-in-death. The book must be carefully kept out of the way of anyone with weak nerves; but for those who can stand it there is a fearful joy in the gradual making clear of the tremendous mysteries involved. The art of the author is of quality high enough *celare artem*. There is no attempt at fine writing, and the simple details almost bring conviction. If they quite brought it, farewell to the reader's peace of mind!

※ ※ ※

43. THE LITERARY WORLD
[LONDON] 57 (FEBRUARY 28, 1898): 167.

NEW NOVELS & NEW EDITIONS
Miss Betty. By Bram Stoker. (C. Arthur Pearson, Ltd. 2s. 6d.) In the last of his previous works, 'Dracula,' Mr. Bram Stoker showed himself a master in the art of weaving blood-curdling plots full of weird imaginings. Very different in his present tale, to which he gives the title *Miss Betty*. Even in 'Dracula' his por-

traiture of women was of the kind we may call tender. Mrs. Harker, it will be remembered, was throughout an adorable person, and so was Lucy until the vampire infected her blood. Betty Pole in the present story is entirely charming, the nearest approach to the angelic that is possible in fiction. [. . .]

✻ ✻ ✻

44. THE HAWKES BAY HERALD [NAPIER, NEW ZEALAND] 23, NO. 10897 (APRIL 23, 1898): 4.

VAMPIRES!
AN UNSUSPECTED DANGER.

I have been reading a book entitled "Dracula." It is a wild, weird thing of surpassing interest, full of historical and psychological research. The author, Mr Bram Stoker, like the "fat boy" in "Pickwick," wants to "curdle your blood"—and he does it. If I jest upon so awful a subject, I should say that this *Stoker couples* an *ingenious train* of thought with many a *tender* passage, that he pays due attention to his "*points*," and his steam at high pressure throughout his work. The plot of the story may be summed up thus: Count Dracula is a professional vampire a great experience, who goes about in the present day sucking the blood of his victims, who in turn become vampires and such other people's blood. He has done this for hundreds of years, but at last Nemesis overtakes him. He is traced to his lair (a box containing concentrated earth from an old burial ground) by a posse consisting of the hero and heroine of the tale, a learned professor (Van Helsig *[sic]*) from Amsterdam, who knows all about vampires, a cute Yankee and a noble lord. The hero opens the box, drives a stake through the heart of the sleeping vampire and cuts off his head, and so kills him for good and all, and thus put it out of his power to do further mischief. A lady of my acquaintance objected to the plot

ARCHIBALD CONSTABLE & CO.

JUST PUBLISHED.
AT ALL THE LIBRARIES AND BOOKSELLERS'.

THE POTENTATE.
A Romance by FRANCES FORBES-ROBERTSON.
THE POTENTATE. Crown 8vo. 6s.

DRACULA. By BRAM STOKER. 6s. Fifth Edition.
"The weirdest of weird tales."—*Punch.*

SIAM—THE KINGDOM OF THE YELLOW ROBE. By ERNEST YOUNG. With 20 Full-page and numerous Text Illustrations. Royal 8vo. 15s.
"Here is a book of which I can speak with unstinted praise......I heartily commend the book."—T. P. O'CONNOR in the *Graphic.*

JUST PUBLISHED.
PREMA-SAGARA; or, THE OCEAN OF LOVE. Translated from the Hindi by F. PINCOTT. Demy 8vo. 15s. net.

SONGS OF LOVE AND EMPIRE. By E. NESBIT. Crown 8vo. 5s. net.
"It is poetry, true poetry, poetry that should live."—*Pall Mall Gazette.*

PROBLEMS OF THE FAR EAST. By the Right Hon. GEORGE N. CURZON, M.P. With numerous Illustrations and Maps. Extra crown 8vo. 7s. 6d.

CONSTABLE, WESTMINSTER.

Constable ad and press notices from The Outlook *1, no. 9 (April 2, 1998): 283. (Image published with permission of ProQuest. Further reproduction is prohibited without permission.)*

that: "it was so unnatural"; but I put it to her: "Did you ever meet a vampire who *was* natural? Why, he couldn't be if he tried, it being his nature to the supernatural."

If this were merely a novel, I should leave it in the hands of the reviewers. But from the discourse of the learned Professor, I gather that vampires are not a fiction of the superstitious brain, but constitute a real though hitherto unsuspected danger; that they exist in our midst, and go about from one country to another, from city to city, pursuing their nefarious practices, and that many deaths, the causes of which have been given up by the faculty at "obscure," may be traced to the ravages of these semi-human semi-diabolical monsters. It is therefore my unpleasant but solemn duty to put the public on their guard. The horrible part of the matter is that young children constitute so large a percentage of the vampire's victims. Mr Bram Stoker's vampire used to put babies into bags, and take them home for the supper of other vampires. It therefore behoves our police to stop all suspicious characters from going about with bags at night. Our author further records cases in which children on Hampstead Heath were waylaid by female vampire (described by them as "a boofler *[sic]* lady"[23]), who began by giving them sweeties, and ended by sucking their blood. Therefore all children who have been out after dark should be examined by the parents of the mark of the vampire bite in the neck. The question is, "What is to be done?" The difficulty of catching a weasel asleep is nothing compared to that of sticking a vampire in a state of somnolence. The faculty are powerless. So is the law, for how can it issue a writ of *ne exeat* against a being who can by occult means leave the kingdom at a moment's notice? It is also obvious that *ca sa* (if it still exists) or a *habeas corpus*, could not be operative in the case of a creature whose corpus you cannot in the first instance catch.

Is there no remedy? I sadly answer: There is no *practical* remedy. But Professor Van Helsig does not abandon us to utter despair. He tells us that there is an unfailing preventive. Vampires can no more abide the smell of garlic than "Trotty Veck" could, by his own account, "abide the smell of bacon." If, therefore, the keyhole and all other crannies in which a vampire could insinuate himself into a bedroom be plugged with these invaluable flowers, its occupant may sleep in peace and safety. This, however, would involve a lack of ventilation, so I suggest a better plan. If the mere flowers of garlic are such a deterrent to the "zoophagi" how much more so would a necklace of the garlic roots be? Nay, more. May we not hope that if everybody would take hearty supper of garlic before going to bed, the human blood would acquire such an aroma that the hungriest vampire would starve sooner than encounter it? Let some of our leading philanthropists try it, and I would bet a £1 note against a Ministerial speech that after that, the mere affixing on the house of a notice: "Vampires Beware! Garlic eaten here," will scare the bloodthirsty wretches away. For some years I have grown garlic, and given it to my neighbors as preventive of distemper in dogs; and people have applied to me for the cloves as a remedy for asthma in old folk, and whooping cough in children. While thus (as I hope) saving valuable lives, canine and human, I had no idea of the extended field of usefulness which I was destined to discover the fragrant herb. I now make the following offer in the cause of suffering humanity:—Let anyone who is worried by vampires apply to me for garlic, and I will freely give it. Those who neglect to avail themselves of this offer must take the fatal consequences. I at least have done my duty.

—*H. H. Murdoch*

※ ※ ※

45. THE LAND OF SUNSHINE [LOS ANGELES] 11, NO. 1 (JUNE 1899): 261.

SUPPED FULL WITH HORRORS

It is economically certain that Mr. Bram Stoker is a sober man. Drunkenness would have no charms, nor delirium any news, for a person of his imagination. His novel, *Dracula*, is a most surprising, affair—and not its least surprise is that of finding yourself clutched and dragged along by so grisly an impossibility. Mr. Stoker has a steady and rather adroit hand to steer and display the paces of his hasheesh fancy; and though the story never convinces, it never loosens its peculiar grip on the reader. "Dracula" is a human vampire—literal vampire of the folkmyths—and with his repellant *motif*, the author has spun a web of horrors I do not remember the mate to. Perforce, all turns out well in the end; else one would have every right to resent so persistent racking of whatever nerves one may have. Doubleday & McClure., New York. $1.50.

—*C. C. Parker*[24]

REVIEWS & REACTIONS   93

***

46. THE PUBLISHERS' WEEKLY [NEW YORK] 1444 (SEPTEMBER 30, 1899): 552.

Stoker, Bram. DRACULA. The author has here produced an exceedingly strong and dramatic story of a human vampire, which has attracted wide attention in England, and as a serial in America. Many competent critics have pronounced it the most daringly successful work of imagination that has seen the light for a long time. It should not be read by people who are afraid of a rather gruesome tale, but those with stronger nerves will surely find it thrilling, and its hold upon the interest is beyond question. [Doubleday & McClure]; Size, 5X71/2; Pages, about 450; Binding, cloth. Price $1.50.

***

47. THE LITERARY WORLD: A FORTNIGHTLY REVIEW OF CURRENT LITERATURE [BOSTON] 30, NO. 20 (SEPTEMBER 30, 1899): 316.

Bram Stoker's *Dracula* will make the reader's hair stand on end.

Dracula
By BRAM STOKER.   *Crown 8vo, 6s.*

" One of the most enthralling and unique romances ever written."—*The Christian World*.
" The very weirdest of weird tales."—*Punch*.
" Its fascination is so great that it is impossible to lay it aside."—*The Lady*.
" The idea is so novel that one gasps, as it were, at its originality. A romance far above the ordinary production."—*St. Paul's*.
" Much loving and happy human nature, much heroism, much faithfulness, much dauntless hope, so that as one phantasmal ghastliness follows another in horrid swift succession the reader is always accompanied by images of devotion and friendliness."—*Liverpool Daily Post*.
" A most fascinating narrative."—*Dublin Evening Herald*.

Press notices for Dracula *from* The Kingdom of the Yellow Robe, *by Ernest Young (Archibald Constable & Co., 1898): 410.*

48. THE SPRINGFIELD REPUBLICAN [MASSACHUSETTS] (NOVEMBER 12, 1899):15.

RECENT WORKS OF FICTION

Bram Stoker, Sir Henry Irving's manager, is engaged in letters as well as in theatrical matters, and has written a blood-curdling romance of vampires and black magic called *Dracula,* which is published by the Doubleday & McClure company. It belongs to the order of "Flames," "The Statement of Stella Maberley," "The Carissima," etc., not to mention such masterpieces as "A Strange Story," "Thrawn Janet," and "The Horla." No doubt Mr. Stoker's fiends are very horrible and obscene, but the story lacks the touch of imagination which is indispensable for producing shudders. Moreover, it is far too long, and although the author has obviated this fault as far as possible by an ingenious use of the Wilkie Collins composite style, the interest is not maintained through so long a stretch of supernaturalism.

* * *

49. DETROIT FREE PRESS (NOVEMBER 18, 1899).

BRAM STOKER'S STORY

It is almost inconceivable that Bram Stoker wrote *Dracula.* Still, he must have done it. There is his name on the title page, and before the tale was bound up and offered us between covers it ran its length in various newspapers,[25] and under the same name of authorship.

So there is no getting around it. Bram Stoker did write it.

Think of the story. It is a tale of ghouls, vampires and human

ARCHIBALD CONSTABLE & CO.

TRAVELS and LIFE in ASHANTI and JAMAN. With many Illustrations from Drawings by the Author, and from Photographs, and 2 Maps. Large demy 8vo. 31s.

The *DAILY CHRONICLE* says:—" The book, with its lively narrative, wealth of description, numerous photographs and sketches, and excellent maps, is more than a mere book of travel."
LE JOURNAL DES DEBATS says:—" Voilà un livre qui, on peut le dire, est arrivé au bon moment, illustré par de très nombreuses photographies et que la Maison Constable a édité avec soin."
The *PALL MALL GAZETTE* says:—" From the Colonial Secretary down to the holiday maker in search of entertaining reading no one who invests in it will be disappointed. Past and future justify the publication of this book—the verdict must be one of unstinted praise."

ON PLAIN and PEAK. Sport in Bohemia and Tyrol. By R. LL. Hodgson.
With 37 Illustrations by H.S.H. Princess Mary of Thurn and Taxis, and from Photographs. Demy 8vo. 7s. 6d.

ENGLISH CONTEMPORARY ART. By R. de la Sizeranne. With Illustrations after Pictures by Lord Leighton, Hubert Herkomer, Sir J. Millais, Burne-Jones, &c. Demy 8vo. 12s.
The *DAILY NEWS* says:—" A brilliant, interesting, and penetrative work......precise and lucid."

UNFORESEEN TENDENCIES of DEMOCRACY. By Edwin Lawrence Godkin. Large crown 8vo. 6s. net.

The *TIMES* says:—" Mr. Godkin is one of the most thoughtful political writers of the day......His experience keeps him in constant touch with public affairs and the contemporary movement of ideas......He writes vigorously and dispassionately, with full knowledge of facts."

MESSRS. ARCHIBALD CONSTABLE & CO. beg to announce that they are now publishing—

The NATURE POEMS of GEORGE MEREDITH. With 20 Full-Page Pictures in Photogravure by William Hyde.

The Edition is limited to 500 Copies for sale in England and America, of which 150 Copies are on Large Hand-Made Paper, and contain an extra Etched Frontispiece signed by the Artist, the price being 5l. 5s. net per vol., whilst of the remaining 350 Copies the price is 2l. 12s. 6d. net per vol.
Prospectus and Specimen Plates may be seen at all the Booksellers'.

TWO NATIVE NARRATIVES of the MUTINY in DELHI. Translated from the Originals by the late CHARLES THEOPHILUS METCALFE, C.S I. (Bengal Civil Service). Demy 8vo. with large Map and 2 Portraits, 12s.

The *SCOTSMAN* says:—" A valuable and substantial contribution, which no student of Indian history can afford to neglect."

DANTE'S TEN HEAVENS: a Study in the 'Paradiso.' By Edmund Gardner. Demy 8vo. 12s.

The *SCOTSMAN* says:—" A valuable addition to any Dante library."
The *DAILY CHRONICLE* says:—" A fascinating and masterly book......His book is an elaborate and erudite exposition of the 'Paradiso.'"

GAIETY CHRONICLES. By John Hollingshead. Profusely Illustrated.
Being a Record of the Gaiety Theatre, the Plays Produced, and Actors and Actresses who have Appeared on its Boards. Demy 8vo. 21s.

The *DAILY TELEGRAPH* says:—" Mr. Hollingshead's comprehensive, interesting, and entertaining book comes exactly at the right time......This well-filled and persuasive volume."
The *REFEREE* says:—" Mr. Hollingshead is the gayest of gay chroniclers......Open the book at any page, and it is like dipping into a lucky-bag, and there are no blanks. Mr. Hollingshead has succeeded in many things, and in these Chronicles he offers as good entertainment as he ever offered."

MESSRS. ARCHIBALD CONSTABLE & CO. will shortly publish—

The LIFE STORY of the LATE SIR CHARLES TILSTON BRIGHT.
Wherein is included the History of the First Transatlantic Cable, and the First Telegraphs to India and the Colonies. By EDWARD BRAILSFORD BRIGHT, and CHARLES BRIGHT, F.R S E. With many Illustrations, Portraits and Maps. 2 vols. demy 8vo. 2l. 2s. net, if ordered before publication, after which the price will be 3l. 3s. net.

PHILIP LAFARGUE'S NEW NOVEL.
STEPHEN BRENT. 2 vols. crown 8vo. 12s.

POPULAR FICTION.

The **POTENTATE**. By Frances Forbes-Robertson. 6s.
The **MACMAHON**. By Owen Blayney. 6s.
DRACULA. By Bram Stoker. Fifth Edition. 6s.
The **DARK WAY** of **LOVE**. By Charles Le Goffic. Translated by Wingate Rinder. 3s. 6d.

imps all in direct communication with Satan. There are lunatics and idiots in it who feed flies to spiders, spiders to sparrows, and then, in lieu of a cat, devour the sparrows themselves. A weird count—the Dracula from whom the book is named—lives in a castle high among the Carpathians and weaves webs for ordinary folk—casts spells over pretty girls, and draws the strings tighter until they die—the girls, that is. An amazing man—Dracula. To achieve his fiendish ends he assumes many and divers forms. Now he is a spirit, visible but untangible, with two sharp front teeth and red eyes. Again he is a dog, then a bat, in turn a wolf at last. As a bat, he goes about biting people in the neck. Of course they die. A Dutch specialist in physiological psychology sets out to solve the mystery of the strange deaths. In the end Dracula is worsted. His head is cut off and a stake is driven through his heart.[26] There's an outline of the tale—such is what you may hope to find between the covers.

And it is a splendid story, too; done in a manner most convincing—by letters, diaries, and medical observations.

And Bram Stoker wrote it!

Think of him.

He—a great, shambling, good-natured, overgrown boy—although he is the business manager of Henry Irving and the Lyceum Theatre—with a red beard, untrimmed, and a ruddy complexion, tempered somewhat by the wide-open full blue eyes that gaze so frankly into yours! Why, it is hard enough to imagine Bram Stoker a business man, to say nothing of his possessing an imagination capable of projecting Dracula upon paper.

But he has done it. And he has done it well.

If you enjoy the weird, if you care for spinal titillations, *Dracula* is unstintingly recommended.

50. NEW-YORK TRIBUNE (ILLUSTRATED SUPPLEMENT) (NOVEMBER 19, 1899): 13.

A FANTASTIC THEME REALISTICALLY TREATED

DRACULA. By Bram Stoker. 12mo, pp. ix, 378. Doubleday & McClure Company. When Victor Hugo said of Beaudelaire that he had added a new shudder to literature he indicated an achievement which countless novelists have since wished to make their own. Most of them have failed. Mr. Bram Stoker has succeeded. "Dracula" is a book of horrors. In some passages the tension is equal to that of the most agonizing nightmare, but the whole work is kept well in hand; consistent from start to finish, it leaves an impression of life and not of mere invention. The author is daring in more ways than one. Choosing a human vampire for the pivot on which his extraordinary drama is to revolve, he has realized that an atmosphere of graveyard mystery must envelope the monster. Those who have read "A Mystery of the Campagna," that clever little story of a vampire by an author who has preferred to remain anonymous, will recall the startling effects which may be gained by an exploitation of the mysterious motive alone. But Mr. Stoker brings Count Dracula from the bleak castle in the Carpathians which shrouds his evil doings in gloom, and turns him loose in England, there to carry out his unspeakable plans amid people and scenes as modern and matter of fact as those of the vampire's mountain home are strange and romantic. The spell of the author's grisly tale is thereby imperilled, but thanks to the skill with which he writes, it remains unbroken. We watch the conflict between Dracula and the group of English people leagued against him with too intense an interest in the amazing spectacle to be at all disconcerted by the impossibilities it involves.

One source of Mr. Stoker's triumph is to be found in the good faith with which he advances his terrible situations. He sets them forth slowly, carefully, with due attention to every little detail, and thus weaves around his hideous central figure a tissue of perfect-

ARCHIBALD CONSTABLE & CO.

POPULAR NOVELS, 6s. each.

The Dominion of Dreams. By FIONA MACLEOD. 6s. *Third Edition.*

In the Shadow of the Crown. By M. BIDDER.

Tattle Tales of Cupid. By PAUL LEICESTER FORD.

The Story of an Untold Love. By PAUL LEICESTER FORD.

Two Fortunes and Old Patch. By T. F. DALE and F. E. SLAUGHTER.

The Old Dominion. By MARY JOHNSTON.

The Puritans. By ARLO BATES.

Dracula. By BRAM STOKER.

Constable ad for Dracula among "Popular Novels" from The Speaker 20, no. 506 (September 9, 1899): 2. (Image published with permission of ProQuest and New Statesman Ltd. Further reproduction is prohibited without permission.)

ly natural things.[27] The honest men who are fighting the vampire may do incredible deeds; they may visit burial vaults at midnight and go through scenes which me must leave Mr. Stoker to describe; but they and their performance are treated with a calm particularity that is in itself impressive and convincing. Then he has considerable ability in the representation of objects and happenings so that the reader really sees them. Witness the account given by Jonathan Harker, one of the characters, of Count Dracula's mode of going about the castle in which the Englishman is temporarily a prisoner:

The window at which I stood was tall and deep, stone-mullioned, and though weatherworn, was still complete; but it was evidently many a day since the case had been there. I drew back behind the stonework, and looked carefully out. What I saw was the Count's head coming out from the window [on the floor below]. I did not see the face, but I knew the man by the neck and the movement of his back and arms. In any case I could not mistake the hands which I had had so many opportunities of studying. I was at first interested and somewhat amused, for it is wonderful how small a matter will interest and amuse a man when he is a prisoner. But my very feelings changed to repulsion and terror when I saw the whole man slowly emerge from the window and begin to crawl down the castle wall over the dreadful abyss, face down with his cloak spreading out around him like great wings. At first I could not believe my eyes. I thought it was some trick of the moonlight, some weird effect of shadow, but I kept looking, and it could be no delusion. I saw the fingers and toes grasp the corners of the stones, worn clear of the mortar by the stress of years, and by thus using every projection and inequality move downwards with considerable speed, just as a lizard moves along a wall.

✻ ✻ ✻

51. THE OUTLOOK: A WEEKLY REVIEW OF POLITICS, ART, LITERATURE, AND FINANCE 63, NO. 13 (NOVEMBER 25, 1899): 738.

BOOKS OF THE WEEK

Dracula. By Bram Stoker. Doubleday & McClure Co., New York. 8vo. 378 pages. $1.50. In another column we notice the appearance of Jókai's "Poor Plutocrats." Mr. Bram Stoker's is also a story of adventure, and is similarly placed as to scene, but there the comparison ends. "Dracula" is a good melodrama of the old-fashioned sort.

✳ ✳ ✳

52. THE BOSTON JOURNAL (NOVEMBER 27, 1899): 5.

THE NEW BOOKS

A GRISLY PHANTASMAGORIA

This is perhaps the grisliest story written in this end of the century. It appeared originally in serial form, but in such a form the full effect of its horrid strength must have been largely missed. Terrible as it is, its power of fascination is so strong that most readers will make an effort to move from beginning to end in a single sitting. Read in this fashion, "Dracula" is a book that enthralls as well as terrifies.

The chief figure in the story, which takes the form of excerpts from the diaries of certain Englishmen and English women, is Count Dracula, a human vampire. The story opens with the arrival at the Castle Dracula, in the midst of the Carpathian Mountains, of Jonathan Harker, a young London solicitor, with whom the Count negotiates for the purchase of a decayed estate near the English metropolis. Harker has not failed to notice that the people roundabout the castle hold the Count in horror, speaking of him in words that they might apply to the devil himself. The castle is a grim place. The Count seems to live alone. He has a forbidding look. His face is vulpine, and at times his eyes sparkle dangerously. Harker tries to cut his visit short, and, bringing things to a point, finds that he is virtually a prisoner. Then, little by little, in a series of gruesome experiences, harker discovers that Dracula is a vampire, that he lives, and has lived for centuries, on human blood.

To make a long story short, Harker escapes, and a few months later both he and the Count, apart from each other, are in London. From this part of the story until the end the reader will hardly pause. The pursuit of the Count, who by day lies bloated with blood in a portable grave and by night, in the shape of a bat, destroys his tender victims, is one of the boldest productions of imagination in modern literature.

The author has done his work artistically. His fancy never becomes absurdity. His Latin is careless, but his carrying of the daring story to a tremendously dramatic conclusion is accomplished faultlessly.

✳ ✳ ✳

53. THE SAN FRANCISCO WAVE (DECEMBER 9, 1899): 5.

THE INSANITY OF THE HORRIBLE

When an Englishman, or, for that matter, anyone of Anglo-Saxon blood, goes into degenerate literature of his own sort, he reveals a horrible kind of degeneracy. The works of the French degenerates possess a verve, a Gaelic attractiveness, indefinable but yet definite, the same subtle quality which, in another line, makes every Frenchwoman, young or old, attractive with a charm that pertains to the soul and not to the body or the mind. Now it

POPULAR NOVELS, 6s. EACH.
THE DOMINION OF DREAMS. By FIONA
MACLEOD. 6s. Fourth Edition.
THE STORY OF AN UNTOLD LOVE. By PAUL
LEICESTER FORD.
THE OLD DOMINION. By MARY JOHNSTON.
DRACULA. By BRAM STOKER. Fifth Edition nearly
Exhausted, Sixth in the Press.

Constable ad for Dracula *among "Popular Novels" from* The Speaker *1, no. 1 (October 7, 1899): xii. (Image published with permission of ProQuest and New Statesman Ltd. Further reproduction is prohibited without permission.)*

goes without saying that the Anglo-Saxon has no such quality. When he becomes degenerate, it is degeneracy of a terrible sort-coarse, brutal, unlovely, its only attraction the fascination of horror. The difference is that between Whitechapel and the Moulin Rouge. I make no doubt that the existence of a Moulin Rouge in its midst is a greater menace to a people than the existence of a Whitechapel, but between the relative attractiveness of the two there is and can be no comparison at all. Swift and Hogarth are two very horrible examples of the Anglo-Saxon method of treating those things which our modern conventionalities decree shall be hidden.

Dracula, by an Englishman who calls himself "Bram Stoker," is an awful example. Here is a man who has taken the most horrible theme he could find in ancient or modern literature, the tradition regarding ghouls, or vampires, the beings, neither living nor dead, who creep in by night to suck the blood and damn the souls of their victims. He has then gone on to carry the thing out to all possible lengths. The plain horror were enough, perhaps, but the author goes farther, and adds insane asylumns, dissecting rooms and unnatural appetites galore. No detail is too nauseating. In the murder, one suicide, one lunatic with homicidal mania and a habit of eating flies, one somnambulist, one shipwreck, extent of fatalities not fully reported, one death by hysterical fright. Pleasant, isn't it? Well, these are only a sort of foretaste of incidents which I, being of a tender conscience, will forbear to harness on the imaginations of others.

There are two reasons of extended mention of this literary failure. The first is that the main cause of the failure shows so prominently as to furnish a beautiful object-lesson. This fault is the lack of artistic restraint. Stevenson, the century's greatest artist in fiction, happens to have used in two instances a theme like this one- in Dr. Jekyll and Mr. Hyde, and on the powerful short story Oliala. And anyone who wishes the lesson should put these two masterpieces, where the horror is suggested, hinted at, written around except for the one moment of the climax when it is brought home with an added force derived from the very fact that it has been hidden so long against this systematic piling-up of all the unwholesome and unpleasant things in the world. The other thing which makes the book worthy of notice is the fact that, in spite of it all, it holds to the end. It is true that the fascination is the same as that which would be possessed by a dissecting room, but it is there nevertheless.

If you have the bad taste, after this warning, to attempt the book, you will read on to the finish, as I did,—and go to bed, as I did, feeling furtively of your throat.[28]

✳ ✳ ✳

54. THE CRITIC: AN ILLUSTRATED MONTHLY REVIEW OF LITERATURE, ART AND LIFE [NEW YORK] 35, NO. 870 (DECEMBER 1899): 1157.

GUIDE FOR THE CHRISTMAS BOOK-BUYER

Dracula, by Bram Stoker, is a most weird and gruesome tale, in which those who love to sup upon horrors will find material for a dozen hearty meals. Count Dracula, the human vampire, is a fiend fit to make the blood of the most hardened horror-lover run cold. The mixture of nineteenth-century fact with mediæval fancy is cleverly done. (Doubleday & McClure, $1.50.)

* * *

55. SAN FRANCISCO CHRONICLE (DECEMBER 17, 1899).

NEW NOVELS AND HOLIDAY BOOKS

One of the most powerful novels of the day and one set apart by its originality of plot and treatment is "Dracula," by Bram Stoker. The author is well known in the dramatic world for his long connection with Sir Henry Irving as manager. Several years ago he wrote a weird story of Irish life, but this is his first long romance. It is a somber study of a human vampire, the Count Dracula, who uses beautiful women as his agents and compasses the death of many innocent people. Theophile Gautier essayed the same subject, but his vampire, who was priest by day and ravening wolf by night, was not half so terrible as this malignant Count with the three beautiful female devils who do his bidding. Nothing in fiction is more powerful than the scene at the killing of the vampire in Lucy's tomb or that other fearful scene at the extinction of the malign power of the Count. The story is told in such a realistic way that one actually accepts its wildest flights of fancy as real facts. It is a superb tour de force which stamps itself on the memory.

* * *

REVIEWS & REACTIONS 105

56. THE ANNUAL AMERICAN CATALOGUE, 1889 [NEW YORK], BY R. R. BOWKER (1900): 207.

Stoker, Bram. Dracula. N. Y., Doubleday & McClure Co., 1899. c. 7+378 p. D. cl., $1.50. A novel originally published in serial form in England.[29] The story is told in the journals of Jonathan and Mina Harker, the diary of one doctor, with the memorandum of another physician, and the notes of Count Dracula, at whose castle in the Carpathian Mountains the gruesome incidents described are supposed to occur. The interest centres in the action of a human vampire. The last scene is tragic.

※ ※ ※

57. THE BROOKLYN DAILY EAGLE (JANUARY 15, 1900): 8.

"DRACULA" OR "THE UN-DEAD"

An Extraordinary Novel by Bram Stoker
—Marvels, and Faith in Them

"Dracula" by Bram Stoker is the name of a book from the pen of the accomplished manager of the Lyceum Theater, London, and of the dramatic companies headed by Sir Henry Irving and Ellen Terry. The publishers are the Doubleday & McClure Company, New York, and the chaste and attractive work of the printer and binder is a worthy setting of the clear thought, the weird imagination and the reverential spirit of a volume of originality, interest and power. The story has been issued both in Great Britain and. America for several weeks, but more than acknowledgment of its appearance has not yet been made in many quarters, for it requires, while it rewards, very careful reading, since its point of view or of treatment is novel, profound and startling.

"The Quick and the Dead"—long before, ages before It was the title of an essentially cheap and brief lived story in these states, the product of erotic fancies and of anaemic thinking—became the comprehensive summary of the two divisions of humanity which, according to the creed, are to be arraigned at the final assize. The term was thought to be all embracing. Mr. Stoker adds to "The Quick or the Dead" a third lot, whom he calls, for want of a better word, the "un-Dead." They comprise the vampire class, if not as a whole, at least as many of them as are affected by a relation to the race of man. The characterization, if not here made for the first time, is for the first time introduced into contemporary fiction for purposes referable to and commendable by religion, and brought by the license of the story' teller within the cognizance of real or presumed medical science. The "un-Dead" are inanimate and powerless by day. They are viciously effective and malignly mobile by night. Of the number of them the book gives neither statement nor intimation. It deals with a housed or castled small colony of them in a mountain fastness of Transylvania, of whom the chief is the Count Dracula, who gives name to the book, "a tall man with a long, brown beard, very bright eyes, which seemed red in the lamplight; a hard-looking mouth. with very red lips and sharp looking teeth, white as Ivory; * * * prodigious strength, his hand actually seemed like a steel vise." Thus he appeared when he whisked the main character up a mountain side to his rocky lair—the proper word is undoubtedly lair. But he is a lightning change artist, and the foregoing description was true of him only when he was acting as his own coachman. In his revealed person, the one in which he figures throughout the book, he is thus described:

> His face was strong—very strong—aquiline, with high bridge of the thin nose and peculiarly arched nostrils, with lofty domed forehead and hair growing scantily round the temples but profusely elsewhere. His eyebrows were very massive, almost meeting over the nose, and with bushy hair that seemed to curl in its own profu-

sion. The mouth, so far as I could see It under the heavy mustache, was fixed and rather cruel looking, with peculiarly sharp, white teeth; these protruded over the lips, whose remarkable ruddiness showed astonishing vitality in a man of his years. For the rest, his ears were pale and at the tops extremely pointed, the chin was broad and strong, and the cheeks firm, though thin. The general effect was one of extraordinary pallor.

Hitherto I had noticed the backs of his hands as they lay on his knees in the firelight, and they had seemed rather white and fine; but seeing them now close to me I could not but notice that they were rather coarse—broad, with squat fingers. Strange to say, there were hairs in the center of the palm. The nails were long and fine and cut to a sharp point. As the count leaned over me and his hands touched me I could not repress a shudder. It may have been that his breath was rank, but a horrible feeling of nausea came over me, which, do what I would, I could not conceal.

The story should better be suggested in large than in little. It is told in the form of journals or letters by the living who are affected by a relation to the "un-Dead." The "un-Dead," by the way, prey on the living, and must recruit themselves from them to accomplish their purpose—which can be described neither as genial nor as friendly. At the opening of the story Count Dracula is completing arrangements for the purchase of real estate in England. A solicitor had had a correspondence with him and had sent on his agent to this mountain retreat to finish the negotiation. The agent's adventures, discoveries, dangers and bare escape are set forth in his journal without the loss of a particular. With his journal, those of his sweethearts at home, of her school friend, of the latter's lover and physician, of that physician's German [sic] medical consultant and of others concur. The scene swings from the mountain retreat to rural England and to London and on the sea, to various ports of touch and back again to the mountain, graveyards, hospitals, country houses, town houses, laboratories, ships, rail trains, transfusion, spells, prayers, all sustaining important parts in the play of purpose. To save the living from the "uh-Dead" and the latter from themselves is that purpose. The former is more difficult than the latter. In fact, the former can not be accomplished except by accomplishing the latter.

Nor is the latter purpose, though easier than the former, of itself easy. The "un-Dead" must, as said, be inanimate in the day time. But that requires them to repose on earth that alone is found in the imaginary mountain retreat. When they Journey, that earth must go as freight on train or ship. O'days on that earth they must lie. O'nights they can be hosts, guests or tourists in the open and freely or furtively in their walks abroad. But the virtue of that earth for them can be neutralized by a sprig of a peculiar sort put on it or by a piece of consecrated wafer! Barring this, however, the "un-Dead" can take the form of bats, flies, cats, birds or what not, and in the night time glut their hideous predatory propensities. To seal up with sprig or wafer all the consignments of earth they freight around is harder than to seal up some. The only effective way is to make the "un-Undead" completely and comfortably dead. That can be done by catching them in their day stupor, by beheading them and by removing and bisecting their hearts! This is progressively done in the ease of every one of the "un-Dead" colony corraled in this book. That done, the poor "un-Dead" are really dead, and no more torment themselves or others. But it is not done without trouble, peril, tragedies, and the like, in which clairvoyance and other occult and pleasing agencies bear no little part. The journals tell it all, and we shall not tell more here.

One is aware that the foregoing suggests what is both grewsome and sensational. It is both, in itself. It suggests itself as neither in a book of which restraint is the keynote of the expression and probability the tone of the improbable or the incredible. Structurally, the severe and even matter of fact veracity of the work is notable and admirable. The impossible, virtual miracles, wonders that eclipse wonder's power to wonder, are told with the precision, moderation, directness and simplicity of Old Testament reporting and well-nigh with its brevity, not to say with its authority, but with the appearance of that authority. The journals are necessarily in the first person, but no writer of them suggests bravado, doubt or consciousness that he may possibly be doubted by others or is "writing for publication." The tone is devout as well as accurate. There are no preludes, no interludes and no postludes—only and always straightaway narrative. The art of it is extraordinary. The art that conceals the art is exquisite. Neither "Kidnapped" nor "Robinson Crusoe" is more outright realistic and honest in its spirit. No stage effects are comparable to these, from which all staginess is absent.

Upon an age of materialism, the book flashes a light of faith. On a time of fade and fakirs, it pours the results of an imagination that is as facile and familiar with marvels as children are made from nurses' lips. If of any legend or old theory the book is an evolution, the secret has been well kept. If it is real for true invention, the persuasive audacity of it is a rare fact and find. None of the characters is above commonplace life in himself, except in his hospitality to the mere things in heaven, earth and hell than are dreamed of in the philosophy of theology or of science. Each is as unconscious of any "'importance" in his work as conduits are of grandeur in carrying to millions of men the refreshment of island springs or of mountain streams. There are romances in the book between the lines, but none in them. There are character studies in the book, but actions are the only letters in which they are written. The work limns the workers. The affection, courage, fortitude, faith, hope, confidence, devotion, piety and altruism that are shown are written in deeds, not in protestations. Even the entrancing accounts of scenery and of incident and of reflections are subsidiary to the one object which is as persistently maintained as fate, and the strokes for and on which are as direct as those of a carpenter on the head of a nail. The noble and humane aim, the delivery into the kindness of complete death of the fell and miserable creatures, the "un-Dead," is the stimulus of the work, as their ineffably sad and diabolical lot is the pathos of the tale.

***

58. THE LITERARY WORLD: A MONTHLY REVIEW OF CURRENT LITERATURE 31, NO. 2 (JANUARY 20, 1900): 26.

DRACULA.

Bram Stoker's *Dracula* is the most exciting old-fashioned story of horrors we have read in a long time. Vampires in modern London, as well as in Transylvania, are prolific of delightful thrills to the sensation lover, and we confess that our favorite among these vampires is the worldly one who resided in Piccadilly and had a card-case; our most vivid imagination had never associated card-cases and vampires, but the two make a weird and attractive combination. The interest of the story is kept up from the first page to the last, and although we should hesitate to recommend Mr. Bram Stoker as a steady literary diet, one feast from him is a relief from the "tendency" and temperamental" fiction of our day and generation. [Doubleday & McClure Co. $1.50.]

***

59. THE TIMES [WASHINGTON] (JANUARY 21, 1900): 8.

A GREWSOME TALE

"Dracula" is a ghost-story by Bram Stoker, who has evidently allowed his imagination full play in its wild and weird incidents. The book has met with favor in England and is now published in book form in America. It will soon appear as a newspaper serial.

The wisdom of putting this story into the newspapers may be questioned from a humanitarian point of view, for the ordinary reader will have to take a nerve tonic after its perusal, especially

REVIEWS & REACTIONS   111

if inclined to timidity, and the newspaper public numbers thousands of nervous and superstitious people, some of whom are imbued with the particular legendary lore from which the conception of "Dracula" originally sprang. The author claims that the idea of the story came to him in a dream, and it is perfectly safe to conclude that the dream was a nightmare.

The central figure of the tale is a human vampire, Count Dracula, a Czech nobleman, who died several hundreds of years ago, and was a remarkable personality in his time. By the uncanny and grewsome processes attributed to the vampire in the folk-lore of various nations, he is supposed to have survived until the present day, and the story begins with the entrance of a young English lawyer into his castle. After seeing some blood-chilling sights, the young man escapes, and returns to England, to find that the foul fiend has migrated to London, and is there engaged in his grisly pursuits in connection with Mina Murray, the lawyer's sweetheart, and a friend of hers named Lucy Westenra. Lucy eventually dies through this means, and a new character comes into the story, a German [sic] physician and scientist, who speaks broken English, and whose language lends a disagreeable air of realism to the incidents, being filled with pseudo-technical term and alarming scientific phrases. At this point there is a curious mingling of sciences, folk-lore, and superstition, and the reader might imagine himself perusing old Cotton Mather's "Magnalia."

The story is told entirely through the medium of letters and journals, and newspaper clippings, another original device which is a stroke of art on the part of the author. All sorts of happenings, apparently unrelated, are introduced one after another and woven into the plot, which gradually becomes more and more complicated as the crisis approaches. The story also becomes more and more like a nightmare. Everyone knows the feeling which comes towards the end of such an experience. There is always a certain avenue of escape toward which the sleeper is vainly striving, and one obstacle after another appears in the way, to be hewn down after seemingly superhuman efforts. The most grotesque circumstances appear natural in the atmosphere of horror and apprehension which envelopes the mind. It is said that once upon a time several well-known writers were comparing notes on drama, and one said that for many years he[30] was troubled by a recurrent dream, which always ended in his awakening, shivering and trembling with terror, in a cold perspiration. When the company begged to know what the vision could have been, he somewhat reluctantly told them. He thought that he "was being chased all over creation by a piece of brown paper."

Some of the incidents Mr. Stoker weaves into his tale are not much more imposing than the brown paper which caused the brilliant author so much agony; but while one is reading the book they seem important and necessary rather than absurd, for the whole thing is put together with consummate skill. It may be that in serial form some of this effect will be lost, for the book is one which, to get the full complement of shivers, ought to be read at a sitting, without a chance to emerge into the full light of day. When one finally closes the book and shakes off the imagery, the whole thing crumbles into nothing, just as did the body of the vampire when the avengers dissected it with their knives. One wonders if the characters themselves did not feel in after years as if the whole thing had been a miasmatic vision of delirium; and the last chapter hints that they did.

Altogether, Mr. Stoker has written a powerful and unpleasant book, and it emphatically ought to be kept out of the way of children of the family, and eschewed by timid people with strong imaginations. (New York: Doubleday & McClure Company. $1.50.)

✳ ✳ ✳

REVIEWS & REACTIONS 113

60. THE INDEPENDENT [NEW YORK] 52, NO. 2667 (JANUARY 11, 1900): 131.

LITERATURE

DRACULA. By Bram Stoker. (New York: Doubleday & McClure Co. $1.00). An ingeniously constructed story, made up out of "documents" which are given the appearance of having been fitted together so as to make a somewhat continuous narrative. Sensational in a mild way, romantic to a degree, and nothing if not picturesque, the story is readable, just the thing for a long evening by a comfortable open fire.

※ ※ ※

61. THE NATIONAL MAGAZINE: AN ILLUSTRATED AMERICAN MONTHLY [BOSTON] 11 (OCTOBER 1899—MARCH 1900): 467-468.

FROM THE CROW'S NEST

Occasionally a book is evolved from the splendid imagination of a master (such must Bram Stoker hereafter be called), the reading of which one recalls with a negative satisfaction, one might almost say with an unpleasing pleasure. "Dr. Jekyll" in his Hyde role, and even the 'umble Uriah Heep, leave one with a shaky faith in human nature, sometimes, though no one can doubt them to be striking characters in fiction, adding much to the literary reputation of their makers. Bram Stoker gives fiction something more unusual than his own name—makes a canvas no one would care to hang, so to speak, in his dining-room, or leave around loose where an imaginative child could view, in the powerful story of a diabolical being known as Count "Dracula," who had the uncanny faculty of drinking other people's blood and thriving thereon. It is at once daring, gruesome, supernatural, wierdly *[sic]* picturesque, and inhumanly engrossing. It is in the form of successive extracts from the journals of Jonathan Harker, of Mina Murray, who became his wife, of Doctors Van Helsing and Seward, and of a woman friend of Mina's, poor Lucy Westenra, who died before heroic efforts to save her could avail. The powers of Darkness come very close to one who reads this book. Should one who prides himself on his nerve test it, that person's flesh will creep, and he will hear strange noises in the night, and he will look sharply into dark corners, and try twice to see that locks are safe before he sleeps. This terrible story of a human vampire is so fraught with strange potions, medical lore and sickroom minutia, and so tingling with dramatic action, that one's head whirls. One thing is quite safe to assume: since the day, not so long ago, when Svengali first became hated by millions, no more horribly realistic character has spread his batswings and flitted across the range of literary vision than Bram Stoker's cruel, fiendish, fascinating Count Dracula, whose hypnotic Nemesis found him, "un-dead" though he was, in the end. England burned midnight oil with the lights turned low, over this remarkable book, and now America, thanks to Doubleday & McClure, may become a part of the universal shudder. Will some one who can sing now kindly strike up that beautiful air which so doubled up Mephistopheles in "Faust," every time that devilish individual heard it?

—*Havre Sacque*

✳ ✳ ✳

62. NEW YORK TIMES (MARCH 17, 1900): 169.

THE WHIMS OF ADVERTISING

What kind of advertising sells books—or does advertising sell books at all? One or two experiences have come to us recently.

[...]

Another case: Mr. Bram Stoker, The gifted Irishman who is

now on a visit to this country, managing the business of Sir Henry Irving, wrote a novel entitled "Dracula," a grim but exciting story of a human Vampire. It had its "first sale" and hung fire. By arrangement it was published as a serial in a New York daily newspaper, the effect of which was immediately to stimulate a large demand not only in New York but all over the Eastern and Western States.

* * *

63. BOOKSELLER & STATIONER [TORONTO, CANADA] 16, NO. 5 (MAY 1900): 7.

WM. BRIGGS' NEW BOOKS

A Canadian edition of Bram Stoker's "Dracula" will appear this month. The author has produced a strong and dramatic story of a human vampire, which has attracted wide attention in England and America. Many competent critics pronounced it the most daringly successful work of imagination that has seen the light for some time. It is not a story for people with weak nerves, who are afraid of the gruesome.

* * *

64. THE NEW YORK TIMES 49, NO. 15.719 (MAY 26, 1900): 345.

"Dracula," too, made its appearance in this interesting list of successful novels in at least one town. This weird and gruesome tale of a human vampire, by Bram Stoker, (Sir Henry Irving's manager,) has attracted much attention as a notable imaginative effort.

SUMMER READING

NATURE BOOKS WITH COLORED PLATES

Dugmore's "Bird Homes." *Just Published.*
3d Thousand. . . . . net, $2.00
Blanchan's "Bird Neighbors." *23d Thousand.* 2.00
Blanchan's "Birds That Hunt and Are Hunted." *10th Thousand.* . . . 2.00
Holland's "Butterfly Book." *5th Thousand. net,* 3.00

SUCCESSFUL NOVELS

Crockett's "The Isle of the Winds." *Just Out.* $1.50
Tarkington's "The Gentleman from Indiana." *43d Thousand.* 1.50
Ollivant's "Bob, Son of Battle." *25th Thousand.* 1.25
Norris's "A Man's Woman." *6th Thousand.* 1.50
Norris's "McTeague." *15th Thousand.* . 1.50
Stoker's "Dracula." *3d Thousand.* . . 1.50
Crockett's "The Black Douglas." *18th Thousand.* 1.50

BY RUDYARD KIPLING

"The Day's Work." *104th Thousand.* . . $1.50
"Stalky & Co." *30th Thousand.* . . 1.50
"From Sea to Sea." *35th Thousand.* . 1.50
"Departmental Ditties and Ballads and Ballads and Barrack-Room Ballads." *25th Thousand.* 1.50

34 UNION SQUARE, EAST, NEW YORK

Ad for Dracula *among "Successful Novels" from*
The Publishers' Weekly, *no. 1478 (May 26, 1900): 1069.*

65. BOOKSELLER & STATIONER [TORONTO, CANADA] 16, NO. 7 (JULY 1900): 2.

WM. BRIGGS' NEW BOOKS

"Dracula," by Bram Stoker, is out in a Canadian edition in very pretty covers. It is a story of dramatic power that will at times make the reader's flesh creep. The scene for the most part is laid among the Carpathian Mountains. . . . This year's book covers are decidedly the prettiest we have seen. The binder's art is taxed to design new and taking designs. Of the newer stories, "The Redemption of David Corson," ["]Philip Winwood" and "Dracula" are exceedingly tasteful and pretty.

* * *

66. THE LITERARY WORLD [LONDON] 62 (SEPTEMBER 14, 1900): 177.

Mr. T. Stoker will have a story entitled "The Pundit," in the October *Pall Mall Magazine*. If we are not mistaken, Mr. Stoker is a retired Indian civilian, who attained to be a distinguished position in the Government of the North-West Province, where the scene of his story is presumably laid. If we are right in our identification he is a brother of Mr. Bram Stoker, who, besides his connection with the Lyceum, has earned considerable fame as a novelist. "Dracula," from his pen, is worthy of E. A. Poe, and is probably the best vampire story extant.[31]

* * *

67. THE LITERARY WORLD [LONDON] 63 (FEBRUARY 22, 1901): 171.

Fiction in the form of letters seems to be having a temporary revival, and anonymity, naturally, is likely to be popular for some time. Mr. Lane is publishing in this form a volume entitled "The Aristocrats," which is said to be written by an aristocrat lady who prefers to reserve her name. The most interesting story we ever read told in this way was Mr. Bram Stoker's "Dracula."

✻ ✻ ✻

68. LLOYD'S WEEKLY NEWSPAPER [LONDON], NO. 3051 (MAY 12, 1901): 11.

Literature

NEW STORIES
Archibald Constable and Co., Ltd.—"Diana of the Crossways," by George Meredith (6d.). "Dracula," by Bram Stoker (6d.). Here we have cheap reprints of two fine novels. The first is one of the finest Irish stories in present day fiction. The second is a romance founded on the superstition of vampirism and as powerful as is weird and uncanny.

✻ ✻ ✻

REVIEWS & REACTIONS 119

69. THE PUBLISHERS' CIRCULAR AND BOOKSELLERS' RECORD OF BRITISH AND FOREIGN LITERATURE [LONDON] 74, NO. 1820 (MAY 18, 1901): 562.

NEW EDITIONS

Messrs. Archibald Constable & Co. have issued a sixpenny edition of Mr. Bram Stoker's "Dracula," one of the most blood-curdling stories that ever came into our hands. For vivid imagination and unrestrained "ghoulism" it would be difficult to surpass it.

* * *

70. THE QUEENSLANDER [BRISBANE, QUEENSLAND, AUSTRALIA] 60, NO. 1335 (JUNE 22, 1901): 1191.

"Dracula," by Bram Stoker (Archibald Constable and Co., sixpenny edition). The latest firm to join the ranks of those who publish sixpenny editions of their copyrighted works is that of Messrs. Archibald Constable and Co., and they have begun well with "Dracula." Nothing Bram Stoker has written has taken greater hold on his admirers than this weird, creepy story of vampires, which he has manage [sic] to invest with so great an air of probability. Issued first in 1897, its success was immediate and considerable. It was just what was wanted by a public always more or less eager after books with spice of superstition and the unknown in them, and as it was cleverly put together, with the theme handled in a peculiarly eery style, they seized on it eagerly, and rejoiced in the cold thrills it sent down their backs. In sixpenny form it will have a still wider circulation, and that large section of the community who delight in ghost stories and all their variants will have an opportunity of gloating over one of the best of the later-day types thereof.

> MESSRS. ARCHIBALD
> CONSTABLE & CO
> LTD beg to announce that they
> are publishing a New Series of
> SIXPENNY EDITIONS
> OF
> COPYRIGHT NOVELS
>
> The first five volumes are as follows:
> GEORGE MEREDITH
> Diana of the Crossways
> Rhoda Fleming
> The Adventures of Harry Richmond
> MARY JOHNSTON
> The Old Dominion
> BRAM STOKER
> Dracula
>
> ARCHIBALD CONSTABLE & CO LIMITED
> 2 WHITEHALL GARDENS WESTMINSTER

Constable ad from With the Flag at Sea, by Walter Wood (Archibald Constable & Co., 1901): 382.

✳ ✳ ✳

71. NELSON EVENING MAIL [NELSON, NEW ZEALAND] 35, NO. 160 (JULY 17, 1901): 2.

AMONG THE BOOKS

Desultorily glancing through older issues the other day one dropped across a very peculiar work by Bram Stoker. One does not know whether to praise it as the most admirable compilation of legend relating to an international superstition, or to condemn it as literature of a most pernicious nature. It is "Dracula," a narrative based on the superstition of the dead-alive, or the vampire. It is a truly awful book, for, even while one laughed at himself for doing it, he was impelled to latch his window when reading it at midnight. Mr Stoker seems to have got hold of every oldwife's tale from all countries, and he has made a curious *olla podrida* of modern science and invention and blood-sucking dead-alives of the Hungarian legend, amongst whom a crusade is successfully instituted by means of the most orthodox methods of the stake through the heart, the garlic garland, and the sacred wafer on the lintel. As a record of ancient superstitions brought down to modern times and made up to date, "Dracula" is very entertaining reading. But it is a book that leaves a painful not to say a fearsome impression, which the perusal of a score of successive and differing works cannot altogether remove. The sixpenny edition is now in circulation.

—M.

※ ※ ※

72. THE STATE [COLUMBIA, SOUTH CAROLINA], PART ONE (AUGUST 4, 1901): 10.

"Dracula," by Bram Stoker. A human vampire is the central figure in this strange story, which has been received with unusual favor in England, and as a serial in America. Many critics have pronounced it the most daringly successful work of imagination of recent years. It may be that to some readers it will prove gruesome, but those of stronger nerves will find in it a thrilling interest that is too genuine to be questioned.

※ ※ ※

73. LONGMAN'S MAGAZINE [LONDON] 38, NO. 228 (OCTOBER 1901): 571-572.

AT THE SIGN OF THE SHIP

[. . .] Thus I have inexpensively perused, and thrown away, Mr. Stoker's *Dracula*. One always heard that it was 'horrid' enough to suit the taste of Ms. Catherine Moreland in *Northanger Abbey*. Yet it only wins a smile from the experienced student of vampires and their ways. The rules of vampiring, as indicated by Mr. Stoker, are too numerous and to elaborate. One does not see why the leading vampire, Count Dracula, could not bolt out of the box where he was finally run to earth by a solicitor named Jonathan. If he could fly about as a bat, why did he crawl down walls head foremost? The rules of the game of Vampire ought to be printed in an appendix; at present the pasttime is as difficult as Bridge. Perhaps I do not understand the rules.

1. Every vampire, all day, must lie in consecrated ground. He can be stumped when *in* his ground, not when out of it.

2. All day a vampire is all-side.

3. No vampire may enter a house uninvited.

4. No vampire may cross salt water except at ebb tide and full tide.

5. Every person bitten by vampire becomes a vampire. (This rule strikes at the root of morality.)

6. No vampire can vamp a person protected by garlic. (The peasantry of Southern Europe always smell of garlic, perhaps as security against vampires.)

7. A vampire, staked through the heart with a sharp piece of wood, is out.

8. Every man should stake his own woman if she is a vampire.

These appear to be the chief rules: there are others to which a person of taste would rather not allude.

* *
*

POPULAR SIXPENNY EDITIONS.

RHODA FLEMING.
By GEORGE MEREDITH.

HARRY RICHMOND.
By GEORGE MEREDITH.

DIANA OF THE CROSSWAYS.
By GEORGE MEREDITH.

DRACULA.
By BRAM STOKER.

THE OLD DOMINION.
By MARY JOHNSTON.

Constable ad for Dracula *among "Popular Sixpenny Editions" from* The Athenaeum, *no. 3848 (July 27, 1901): 137. (Image published with permission of ProQuest and New Statesman Ltd. Further reproduction is prohibited without permission.)*

On the whole, *Dracula* is very much too 'bluggy,' and that not as the result of honest clash of steel. The girl who became a vampire after receiving three proposals in one day must have been a minx. She went about vamping children at Hampstead. A vampire with a cheque-book, a solicitor, and a balance at the bank, is not a plausible kind of creature. Mr. Sheridan LeFanu's Carmilla was a better and more credible vampire, and her story was less butcherly than this sixpence narrative. To me the vampire belief seems one of the very few superstitions which have not a basis in fact of some kind; unless, indeed, the basis is the nature of infectious diseases.

—Andrew Lang

✱ ✱ ✱

DRACULA.
By BRAM STOKER.
Sixth Edition. Crown 8vo, 6s.

"In seeking a parallel to this weird, powerful and horrible story, our minds revert to such tales as 'The Mysteries of Adolpho,' 'Frankenstein,' 'Wuthering Heights,' 'The Fall of the House of Usher," and 'Marjery of Quelher.' But 'Dracula' is even more appalling in its gloomy fascination than any one of these."—*Daily Mail.*

"It is horrid and creepy to the last degree. It is also excellent, and one of the best things in the supernatural line that we have been lucky enough to hit upon."—*Pall Mall Gazette.*

Press notices for Dracula *from* Dante and Giovanni del Virgilio, *ed. Philip Henry Wicksteed and Edmund Garratt Gardner (Archibald Constable & Co., 1902): 367.*

74. A CUMULATED INDEX TO THE BOOKS OF 1901 [MINNEAPOLIS] 4, COMPILED BY M. E. POTTER (1902): 571.

Stoker, Bram. *Dracula.* (Pan-American lib., no. 6.) D. 9-378p. 50¢. (c.'97.) '01. Wessels. A gruesome story told in Jonathan and Mina Harker's journals, the diary of the Doctor Seward, and a memorandum by another physician. The scene is laid in the Carpathian Mountains at the castle of Count Dracula, an uncanny monster of wickedness. The story was published by Doubleday, Page & Co. in 1899.

✳ ✳ ✳

75. DETROIT TRIBUNE (JANUARY 24, 1902).

Known merely as the astute manager of Sir Henry Irving's interests, Bram Stoker is a writer of renown. His *Dracula,* a weird story of a human vampire, is as vivid and thrilling as [Poe's] 'The Black Cat' with vastly more detail.

76. THE BOSTON HERALD (APRIL 6, 1902): 36.

ACTOR-MANAGER AND AUTHOR

Of these [Stoker's books] "Dracula" is by far the best known here. It was published by the Harpers [sic] and in a serial form by the New York Sun, and more than a year later by a syndicate of newspapers. The story is that of a human vampire, and the author's power to make the seemingly impossible seem real is extraordinarily convincing. Some descriptions of scenery in the wildest country of the Danubian banks are written with a true painter's insight.

※ ※ ※

77. THE SPRINGFIELD REPUBLICAN (APRIL 6, 1902): 19.

BOOKS, AUTHORS AND ARTS

BRAM STOKER'S NEW ROMANCE

Bram Stoker has accomplished no small achievement in "The Mystery of the Sea" (Doubleday, Page & Co). He has made the Baconian "bi-lateral cipher," so inexpressibly dreary in the hands of Mrs Gallup and her kind, a source of real entertainment. Bram Stoker is well known in this country, not merely as the author of "Dracula," as weird and ghastly a tale as has been penned in recent years, but as the manager of Sir Henry Irving, in which capacity he has made friends in most cities of the United States, while is Herculean form is familiar to theater-goers wherever Sir Henry and Miss Terry have appeared. He has had a varied and remarkable career, and it is surprising he should have been able to find time to produce so much fiction, and of a quality quite out of the ordinary. "The Water's Mou" *[sic]* was a simple and tragic little romance of the sea-coast and the fisher-folk. "Dracula" was a very singular and imaginative tale of a modern vampire, a hideous power of darkness which came from the mountain wilds of Austria *[sic]* and invaded the commonplace and prosaic air of London. It was too long-drawn-out, and there were too many chests of devil's dust to be hunted down and destroyed, but it was a story of so unusual and original a sort that no one who read it is likely to forget it.

✲ ✲ ✲

78. BOOK NEWS: A MONTHLY SURVEY OF GENERAL LITERATURE [PHILADELPHIA] 20 (OCTOBER 1902): 125.

DRACULA. By Bram Stoker. A reprint in less expensive shape of "Dracula," a novel which appeared in 1897. It has since been reprinted in a number of daily newspapers, and constitutes, on the whole, the most remarkable story of mystery and horror which has appeared in many years. The Pan-American Library. 378 pp. 12mo. Paper.

✲ ✲ ✲

79. THE OXFORD POINT OF VIEW 1, NO. 3, EDITED BY M. COMPTON MACKENZIE (OCTOBER 1902): 208.

THE PILE OF BOOKS

[. . .] When *Dracula* first appeared I read it with terror, and was afraid to look behind me for several days. Later on I saw it in

Cover for the abridged, trade paperback edition of Dracula *(Archibald Constable & Co., 1901).*

cheap edition with a silly picture of a deformed acrobat on the cover, and the fascination of the book was gone. The excuse so often urged, that these cheap editions help the appreciation of good literature by bringing good authors within the reach of the most modest means, is balderdash. The position of charitable patrons of learning which so many publishers affect, ceases when their pockets are touched: they cheapen the market and themselves with equanimity so long as they avoid cheapening their account at the bank. While novels are looked upon in the same way as saucepans, it will become more difficult each year to find any fit to read, still less to keep

❋❋❋

80. THE AUGUSTA CHRONICLE [GEORGIA] (JULY 9, 1905): 2.

LITERARY NOTES

READ AND REVIEWED

IN THE LIBRARY

[. . .] We are told if we investigate with fair mind the evidence for ghosts, the belief will be established. Perhaps the same is true of vampires.

Impalpable but real, hovering on the borderland—that indenable line between the spiritual and material—the dehumanized vampire is a thing passed the imagination of poets, more bloodcurdling than any demon of Dante's "Inferno." Those initiated into the horrors of "Dracula" say to their friends—"Do not read it at night." Perhaps the ominous warning lends to break the spell the author would cast about the reader. The present writer reads "Dracula" at night without a tremor. Perhaps, after Poe, one is inured to the story of terror. It goes without saying that talented

Bram Stoker has not the genius of Poe, or one could not easily escape the magic spell. If Poe had portrayed the vampire as vividly as he did the Black Cat, it would have been enough to wreck any nerve.

"Dracula" is weird, harrowing, spellbinding, no doubt, to many, but to one who will think and not give up to feeling, it is but an interesting study in the so-called supernatural; not literature in the best sense, with its verisimilitude of faithful chronicling and detective work; and it will, no doubt, "go to storage" along with other books of the times. When it comes to light again, will we wonder, as of Henry Brocke's "The Good quality," how ought so trite and simple could ever seemed *[sic]* daring and past credulity?

Surely, we are not on the road to finding Vampires so commonplace.

The story of "Dracula" owes its fascination in part to the contrasts of English life and character, loved and lover, with the antithesis of all good and wholesome in the remote, dreary, haunted ruins of castle Dracula, in the Carpathian mountains, where dwelt the evil Thing-ghost, blood-sucking demon—Dracula. The connection of legendary beliefs with established fact—gossamer though it be—may be traced somewhere under all the legends of vampire and were-wolf, of fairies and phantoms, lies a truth, but whether or not it is ever revealed in trustworthy evidence, we cannot venture to say. The present writer was given the privilege by the librarian of the Young Man's Library of seeing an artistic conception of Dracula, the Terrible, drawn by a gifted young Augustan. It illustrates the scene where the lithe, black Thing of flaming eyes and red—too red lips drawn over white pointed cruel teeth, is found bending over lovely Lucy, as she lies prostrate at the midnight hour on the lonely tombstones. What can be more hideous than this vampire drawing from young veins the life blood—the very soul—of a pure and gentle maiden? It is a subject worthy of Poe's pen, of the artist's pencil. We know that the dark regions exist, but why look into the depths?

There is white magic as well as black—and sweetness and light

FICTION.
Crown 8vo. 6s. each Volume.

MR. HENRY JAMES'S GREAT NOVEL.

THE WINGS OF THE DOVE.

" Mr. Henry James is to be congratulated. It is a long time since modern English fiction has presented us with a book which is so essentially a book ; a thing conceived, and carried on, and finished in one premeditated strain ; with unbroken literary purpose and serious, unflagging literary skill."—*Times.*

THE WINGS OF THE DOVE.

" In the beauty of its style, in the raciness of its emotional quality, in the orderly evolution of its theme, in the fine handling of its principal characters, the book seems to us to be upon the highest level even of its author's attainments."—*Academy.*

THE WINGS OF THE DOVE.

" ' The Wings of the Dove ' is a novel which everybody ought to read."—*World.*

THE WINGS OF THE DOVE.

One gets out of a novel by Mr. James more moral, emotional and intellectual delights than out of hundreds of banal novels.
" I feel bound to pay in praise for the exquisite pleasure which Mr. James provides. I do not complain because he provides a new kind of pleasure, a pleasure differing from the pleasure provided by Dickens."—Mr. JAMES DOUGLAS in the *Star.*

THE WINGS OF THE DOVE.

" Many beauties of thought, language and characterisation distinguish Mr. Henry James's latest and perhaps most brilliant novel."—*To-day.*

THE FORERUNNER.
The Romance of Leonardo da Vinci.
By MEREJKOWSKI,
Author of " The Death of the Gods."

" A novel of very remarkable interest and power. Full of beautiful passages which one is tempted to quote."—*Guardian.*
" A very powerful piece of work, standing higher above the level of contemporary fiction than it would be easy to say."—*Spectator.*
" This superb romance."—*World.*
" One of those books which takes the reader by assault ; one feels the impulsion of a vivid personality at the back of it all."—*Academy.*

MISS JOHNSTON'S FAMOUS NOVELS.

AUDREY. [4th Edition.
BY ORDER OF THE COMPANY. [12th Edition.
THE OLD DOMINION. [8th Edition.

DRACULA.
By BRAM STOKER.
[7th Edition.

dispel the powers of darkness. If we might believe in vampires, let us believe in angels too—guardian angels—who are potent against evil.

"The myriad-minded Shakespeare" believed in both Caliban and Artel; yes, and in witches, ghosts and fairies. This is an age of many various beliefs. Those who can believe in only a few little things are rated among the ignorant and superstitious.

The superstitious are those who cannot believe in fairies, said some one the other day.

To try your nerve and credulity—read "Dracula!"

—H. M. L.

✳✳✳

81. THE REGISTER [ADELAIDE, SOUTH AUSTRALIA] 70, NO. 18,354 (SEPTEMBER 9, 1905): 12.

FOR STRONG NERVES ONLY

[. . .] Mr. Bram Stoker's "Dracula" is the touchstone by which all modern "creepy" stories must be tried. Mr. Benson's books falls *[sic]* short of that high standard only because it makes the reader feel that death after all can end any sufferings. In "Dracula" death is never a stepping-stone in the progress of horrors. "The Image in the Sand" can be read without resulting discomfort by any person of fairly strong nerves.

✳✳✳

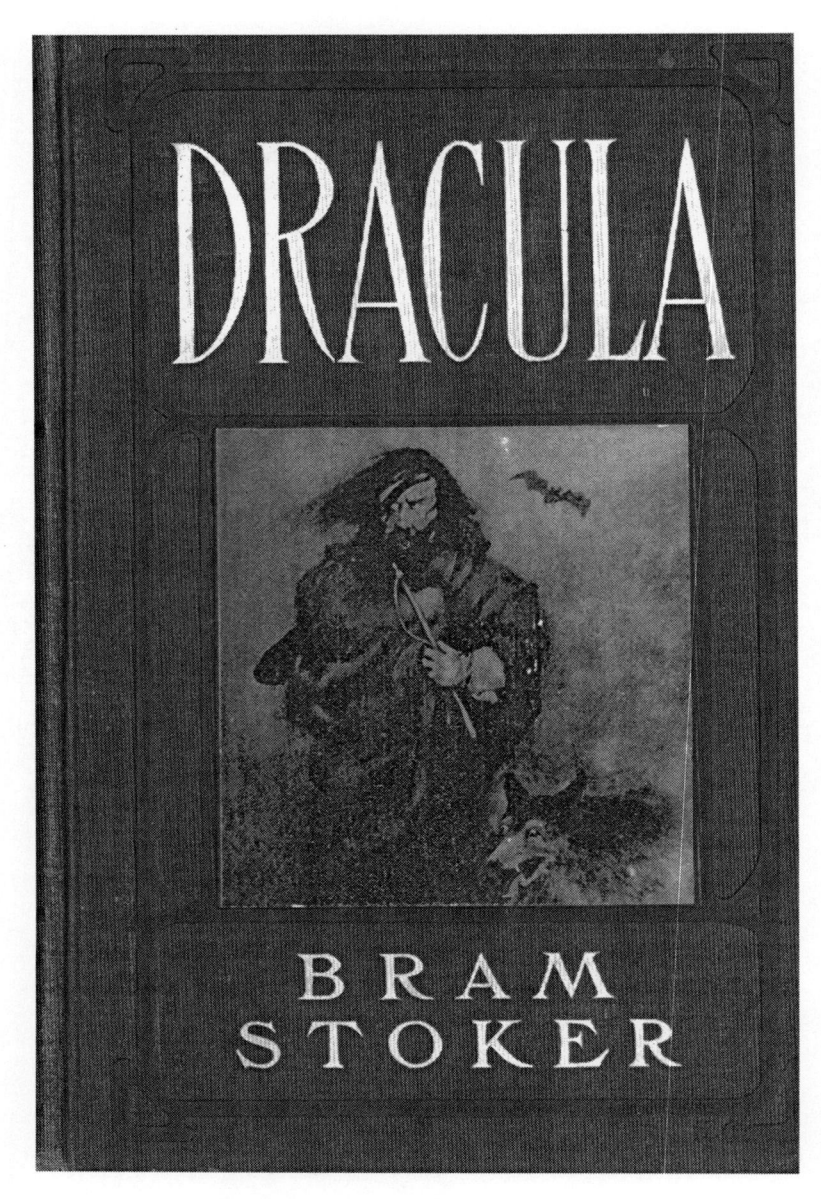

Cover for the fourth American edition of Dracula *(Doubleday, Page & Co., 1902). Courtesy of Patrick MacDanel.*

82. THE SKETCH (OCTOBER 24, 1906).

Predicted that *Dracula* would be "reprinted in the cheap series of 2000 A. D."

* * *

83. MARLBOROUGH EXPRESS [BLENHEIM, NEW ZEALAND] 43, NO. 260 (NOVEMBER 2, 1909): 3.

ITEMS OF INTEREST

[. . .] One of the most curious legacies ever bequeathed to anybody is perhaps that of £1000 left by the late Mrs Olivia Flint, of Pittsburg, to her doctor. Mrs Flint was very fond of novel reading, and, although very ill, began to read Bram Stoker's thrilling romance, "Dracula." So interested did the dying woman become in it, that when she had read a chapter or two, she turned to her nurse, and, asking for pen and ink, wrote a few words to the effect that if Dr Allardyce could keep her alive long enough for her to finish the tale he was to receive a legacy of £1000. Mrs Flint lived for several hours after the last words had been read.

* * *

84. THE KANSAS CITY STAR 32, NO. 7 (SEPTEMBER 24, 1911): 1.

AMONG THE BOOKSMITHS

[. . .] Speaking of tales of terror, did you ever read "Dracula," by Bram Stoker, the former manager and friend of Henry Irving? Nobody, having read it, will ever forget it. The gloomiest and most morbid of Poe's stories seem harmless and soothing by com-

SIX-SHILLING FICTION.

"A GREAT LITERARY TRIUMPH."

SIR MORTIMER. By Mary Johnston. Illustrated by F. C. YOHN.

"My Nautical Retainer desires once again to acknowledge his indebtedness to Mary Johnston, author of that fascinating story 'By Order of the Company.'..... The author from the very outset has the reader almost mercilessly in thrall.....As noble a picture of loyalty in love as you will find in any page of English romance.....It is a book of which she has every right to be proud; and, indeed, when one reflects upon the proofs here given of her possession of those qualities so rarely found together—a man's strength and a woman's tenderness—it would be hard to name a living writer who could have written it for her."—*Punch.*

"Miss Johnston has achieved a great literary triumph..... It is a fine tale, ingeniously constructed, full of imagination, and rich with insight of the aspirations of Elizabethan England."—*Daily Chronicle.*

"Miss Johnston realizes for us a creation of real power and charm..... The tragic fortunes of Sir Mortimer Ferne will be followed with an absorbing interest."—*Globe.*

BY THE SAME AUTHOR.

AUDREY. THE OLD DOMINION.
BY ORDER OF THE COMPANY.

SECOND EDITION NOW READY.

DOROTHEA. A Story of the Pure in Heart. By Maarten Maartens.

ENID. By Marmaduke Pickthall, Author of 'Said the Fisherman.'

BROKE of COVENDEN. By J. C. Snaith, Author of 'Mistress Dorothy Marvin,' &c.

MR. LIONEL CUST'S NEW BOOK.

ANGELO BASTIANI. A Story of Modern Venice. By LIONEL CUST. With many Illustrations by FRANK H. MASON, R.B.A. Crown 8vo, cloth gilt.

A NEW BORDER ROMANCE.

MAGNUS SINCLAIR. By Howard Pease, F.S.A., Author of 'Borderland Studies,' 'The Mark o' the Deil,' &c.

"Mr. Pease has written a very vigorous and racy book......'Magnus Sinclair' is a capital book of its kind, racy and invigorating."—*Speaker.*

"The story is a pleasant one, full of exciting episodes."—*Saturday Review.*

"This is an able and interesting......historical romance."—*Scotsman.*

CONSTABLE'S 2s. 6d. SERIES.

POPULAR COPYRIGHT NOVELS NOW READY.

Small crown 8vo, cloth gilt, 2s. 6d. net.

CARDIGAN. By R. W. Chambers, Author of 'Maids of Paradise,' 'Ashes of Empire,' &c.

DRACULA. By Bram Stoker, Author of 'The Jewel of Seven Stars,' &c.

Constable ad for Dracula among "Six-Chilling Fiction" from The Athenaeum, no. 4002 (July 9, 1904): 64. (Image published with permission of ProQuest and New Statesman Ltd. Further reproduction is prohibited without permission.)

parison. It is a masterpiece of its kind, and the author must have soaked himself with ghostly legends to be able to write it. The yarn is based on the old Hungarian superstition of vampires, dead people who prey upon the living, and some of the incidents of the story are the very concentration of ghastly terror. A newspaper story, current three or four years ago, said that a young Englishman became a raving maniac after reading "Dracula," and that is not hard to believe. Fortunately, Stoker has quite that line of literary effort, or he might contribute largely populating the booby hatches. An average man can read one story of the kind and retain his reason, but a course of such stuff would be fatal. Stoker's latest book treated of celebrated imposters of different ages, and one chapter of it was extremely interesting, as it furnished a lot of plausible evidence showing that Queen Elizabeth was in reality a man. Stoker must have done a vast amount of work to gather the material for that chapter, and so the story has its value. "Dracula" has its value for the same reason. It is the outcome of tireless research and it sheds much light upon one of the fascinating, though ghostly, superstitions of a strange people.

—*Walt Mason*

* * *

85. THE OUTLOOK: A WEEKLY REVIEW OF POLITICS, ART, LITERATURE, AND FINANCE 30 (1912): 704.

Dracula, by Bram Stoker (William Rider, ninth edition, 1s. net).—The lamented death of the author should direct fresh attention to the most imaginative creation of his pen. For weird force and picturesque horror *Dracula* deserves to rank with the classics of morbidity. The publisher has been well advised to issue the story at a price which should assure it a wide public welcome. The binding and letterpress are notable even in these days of cheap production

86. THE NEW YORK TIMES (APRIL 26, 1912): 10.

BRAM STOKER'S STORIES
To the Editor of the New York Times:
May I voice a mild dissent from your rather slighting editorial reference to Bram Stoker's stories? "Dracula" will always held in high esteem by all lovers of the horrible as one of the most delightfully blood-curdling hair-raisers ever written.

JANE PENNIMAN.[32]
New York, April 23, 1912.

✳ ✳ ✳

87. THE BOOKMAN: A MAGAZINE OF LITERATURE AND LIFE 35, NO. 4 (JUNE 1912): 347-348.

CHRONICLE AND COMMENT
"FRANKENSTEIN"
Since the death of Bram Stoker several writers in the weekly and daily journals have thought to bestow high praise upon his *Dracula* by saying that it will eventually take its place with Mrs. Shelley's *Frankenstein*. We wonder how many of these writers have read *Frankenstein*, which, despite the fact it is remembered after one hundred years, is one of the most badly constructed and written stories. When the voice of pessimism over the degenerate library conditions of our time is particularly loud we can console ourselves with the thought that *Frankenstein*, in the form in which it was written, could not be published to-day. There is probably hardly a "publicity" man in any of our leading American publishing houses who could not be trusted to edit and "touch it up" to good effect. At any rate there could be very little harm done by revision.

6s. SUMMER FICTION. 6s.

SIR MORTIMER.
By MARY JOHNSTON.
Illustrated by F. C. YOHN.
"Miss Johnston has achieved a great literary triumph. . . . It is a fine tale, ingeniously constructed, full of imagination, and rich with insight of the aspirations of Elizabethan England."—*Daily Chronicle.*

BY THE SAME AUTHOR.
"AUDREY,"
"BY ORDER OF THE COMPANY,"
"THE OLD DOMINION."

MAGNUS SINCLAIR.
A Border Historical Novel.
By HOWARD PEASE.
"A very vigorous and racy book."—*Speaker.*
"Full of exciting episodes."—*Saturday Review.*

THE DIVINE FIRE.
By MAY SINCLAIR,
Author of "Two Sides of a Question," "Mr. and Mrs. Nevill Tyson," &c.

ARCHERS OF THE LONG BOW.
By ARTHUR MOORE,
Author of "The Knight Punctilious," &c. [*Shortly.*

PATHS OF JUDGMENT.
By ANNE DOUGLAS SEDGWICK. [*Shortly.*

THE BANDOLERO.
By PAUL GWYNNE,
Author of "Marta." [*Shortly.*

VERANILDA.
By GEORGE GISSING,
Author of "The Private Papers of Henry Ryecroft," &c.
[*Shortly.*

BROKE OF COVENDEN.
By J. C. SNAITH,
Author of "Mistress Dorothy Marvin," &c.
"He possesses the rare faculty of writing witty and incisive dialogue and of conceiving and describing powerful scenes."—*Daily News.*

ENID.
By MARMADUKE PICKTHALL,
Author of "Saïd the Fisherman."
"The qualities which made Said so brilliant a book are all to be found in its successor. The characterisation of 'Ænid' is clear and various."—*Athenæum.*

DOROTHEA.
A Story of the Pure in Heart.
By MAARTEN MAARTENS. [*2nd Edition.*

ANGELO BASTIANI:
A Story of Modern Venice.
By LIONEL CUST.
With many Illustrations by FRANK H. MASON, R.B.A.

CONSTABLE'S 2s. 6d. SERIES.
Small crown 8vo, cloth gilt, 2s. 6d. net.
POPULAR COPYRIGHT NOVELS.
NOW READY.

CARDIGAN.
By R. W. CHAMBERS,
Author of "Maids of Paradise," "Ashes of Empire," &c.

DRACULA.
By BRAM STOKER,
Author of "The Jewel of Seven Stars," &c.

Constable for Dracula among "Summer Fiction" from The Speaker *(July 16, 1904): 365. (Image published with permission of ProQuest and New Statesman Ltd. Further reproduction is prohibited without permission.)*

Dracula, by the way, had some curious vicissitudes in the United States. At first no American publisher would take it and Bram Stoker himself went to considerable expense in copyrighting it in this country. Time went on, and it looked as if this money—hard-earned, as was all Stoker's money—would be utterly wasted. Then suddenly a publisher took the book, and from the very first its sales were enormous, not only in the States, but in Canada also.

* * *

88. THE ACADEMY AND LITERATURE 82, NO. 2092 (JUNE 8, 1912): 721.

Dracula. By Bram Stoker. (William Rider and Son). The new issue of "Dracula," by Bram Stoker, constitutes the ninth edition of that weird story, and the publishers have presented it very creditable form. It is well bound and clearly printed, and those who have not read one of the most uncanny stories of modern times, perhaps, that ever was written, should purchase it in this cheap reissue without delay.

* * *

89. THE ATHENAEUM [LONDON], NO. 4410 (MAY 4, 1912): 502.

Stoker (Bram), DRACULA, 1/ net. Rider. The ninth edition of this eerie extravaganza. It is a skilfull experiment in the horrible, though its "curdling" is carried to excess. Throughout the author displays an extraordinary inventiveness and manipulation of effects.

REVIEWS & REACTIONS

* * *

90. THE NEW YORK HERALD (JULY 6, 1912): 6.

Among the notices on the death of Bram Stoker not many make any mention of his book "Dracula," and although it has sold well, comparatively few people seem to have read it. It deals with the habits of that fabulous being the vampire, and to those who have not outgrown the delight of having their flesh creep it may be recommended as a book second only in thrills to some Edgar Poe's weirdest tales.

* * *

DEATH OF BRAM STOKER.

Abraham (Bram) Stoker, long time business-manager of the London Lyceum and chief assistant to the late Sir Henry Irving there and on his American tours, died in London on April 21, aged fifty-four years. He was born in Dublin, was graduated from Trinity College there, where he was athletic champion, and was called to the English bar. Then he became dramatic, art, and literary critic for London and Irish papers, joining Mr. Irving in 1878. He was author of many novels, more or less sensational, and his "Personal Reminiscences of Henry Irving," published in 1906, ranks as perhaps the most comprehensive summary of the career of the great actor-manager.

After Sir Henry's death, Mr. Stoker joined the staff of the London *Daily Telegraph* and later managed the tour of David Bispham in The Vicar of Wakefield. He married Florence Anne Lemon Balcombe, who survives with a son, and he was a medallist of the Royal Humane Society.

Obituary of Bram Stoker from The New York Dramatic Mirror *(May 1, 1912): 12.*

Rider ad and press notice for Dracula *among "Rider's Latest Fiction" from* The Playgoer and Society Illustrated *7, no. 42 (March 1913): 11. (Image published with permission of ProQuest. Further reproduction is prohibited without permission.)*

91. A GUIDE TO THE BEST FICTION [NEW YORK] NEW ED., BY ERNEST A. BAKER (1913): 357.

Stoker, Bram [1847-1912]. Dracula. 1897. A very successful handling of horrible sensations in a realistic way—a Gothic romance adapted to the more exacting requirements of *fin-de-siècle* readers. A terrible baron in a Transylvanian castle is the chief of an army of human vampires that prey on mankind and pursue their ravages as far as London, demanding all the determination and resource of the hero and his friends to exterminate them. [2s. 6d. n., Constable; $1.50, Doubleday, New York; 50¢., Wessels, New York.]

Rider's Popular Fiction

Uniform with 'DRACULA.' Small crown 8vo. cloth gilt, 1s. net each volume.

Just Published.

THE LADY OF THE SHROUD.
By BRAM STOKER.
"A wild and whirling romance no less fascinating than his first horribly grim story of 'DRACULA.'"
Daily Telegraph.
"One is left aghast at the fertility of Mr. Stoker's imagination and the vigour of his pen."—*World.*

DRACULA. By BRAM STOKER.
"The very weirdest of weird tales."—*Punch.*

THE MYSTERY OF THE SEA.
By BRAM STOKER.
"To any one who loves an enthralling tale told with unflagging zest and good spirits we recommend 'The Mystery of the Sea.'"—*Pall Mall Gazette.*

THE JEWEL OF SEVEN STARS.
By BRAM STOKER.
"In mystery and interest the book is thrilling, and at times sensational."—*Daily Graphic.*

Rider ad and press notice for Dracula *among "Rider's Popular Fiction" from* The Athenaeum, *no. 4523 (July 4, 1914): 4. (Image published with permission of ProQuest and New Statesman Ltd. Further reproduction is prohibited without permission.)*

Cover for Dracula, l'homme de la nuit *(L'Édition française illustrée, 1920), the first French edition of* Dracula.

BIBLIOGRAPHICAL AFTERWORD: NON-ENGLISH EDITIONS OF DRACULA

J. Gordon Melton

Through the twentieth century, to the present, *Dracula* has been translated into a number of languages. Only two such editions, one in Icelandic and one in German, appeared during Stoker's lifetime, but in the 1920s, editions appeared in French, Italian, and Spanish. There was a dramatic increase in the number of translations after *Dracula* went into the public domain in the 1960s, due in part to the popularity of the title character in the movies and in part to the use of *Dracula* as a reader for the teachings of English. A new wave of editions appeared in 1979 when the Frank Langella *Dracula* was released.

A number of translations into Eastern European languages were made in the 1990s after the fall of the Soviet Union. These were partially inspired by the 1992 release of Francis Ford Coppola's movie, *Bram Stoker's Dracula*. Since the beginning of the new century, editions have appeared in Russian, Ukrainian, and most recently in Chinese.

The list below is organized by language rather than country. Thus, editions from South America and from Spain will be found under Spanish, and a similar arrangement was made for Portuguese editions. French editions include those published in Belgium, Switzerland, and Quebec. In addition to the full translations of *Dracula*, where applicable we have listed the abridged editions, both those issued for the juvenile market and those for teaching language, and the graphic arts comics editions.

The compiler of this list is most interested in learning of other editions of *Dracula* in additional languages. Information on such editions may be sent to jgordon@rain.org.

Chinese

Turvey, John, adapted by. *Dracula*. London: Longman Group UK Limited, 1999. 112 pp. pb. Cover: Louis Jourdan as Dracula. Bilingual English-Chinese edition licensed for sale exclusively in the People's Republic of China.

Vaughn, Susan, adapted by. *Dracula*. Taipei: Amen, 2001. 223 pp. tp. Bilingual Chinese/English edition.

Czech

1970 *Dracula*. Trans by Tomás Korbar from the 1966 Jarrolds ed. Prague: Odeon, 1970. 365 pp.

1991 *Dracula*. Trans by Tomás Korbar. Práce: Mistral, Edice Dobré Cetby, 1991. 247 pp. Pb. Illustrated by Theodor Rotrekl.

Dracula. Trans by Tomás Korbar. Práce: Prace, 1991. 247 pp. Illustrated by Zbynik Hraba.

Danish

1963 *Drakula*. Trans. by Benny Andersen. Copenhagen: Borgen, 1963. 396 pp. Series: Borgens Billigborgen, 14. Reprinted: 1970, 1973.

1970 *Drakula*. Trans. by Benny Andersen. Copenhagen: Borgen, 1970. 396 pp. Series: Borgens Billigborgen, 14.

1973 *Drakula*. Trans. by Benny Andersen. Copenhagen: Borgen, 1973. 396 pp. Series: Borgens Billigborgen, 14.

1989 *Drakula*. Trans. by Benny Andersen. Copenhagen: Borgen, 1989. 396 pp.

1990 *Drakula*. Trans. by Thornsten Villum Hansen and Niels Krohn. Copenhagen: Forum, 1990. 213 pp.

BIBLIOGRAPHICAL AFTERWORD 145

1993 *Drakula.* Trans. by Benny Andersen. Copenhagen: Borgen Paperback, 1973. 396 pp. pb. Cover: from Bram Stoker's Dracula.

1998 *Drakula.* Trans. by Benny Andersen. Copenhagen: Borgen, 199873. 396 pp. Series: Borgens Klassiker.

Danish Adaptation
1991 Trans. by Thornsten Villum Hansen and Niels Krohn of an original text by Wendy Hobson. Copenhagen: Junior Bogklubben, 1991. 137 pp.

Dutch
1973 *Dracula.* Trans. by Else Hoog. Deure: Brune & Zoon, 1973. 384 pp. Series: Zwarte beerjes, 18.

1980 *Dracula.* Trans. by Else Hoog. La haye: Nederlandse Boekenclub, 1980. 392 pp. Book club edition.

1992 *Dracula.* Trans. by Jose de graaf. Baarn: In den toren, 1992. 302 pp. Series: Tioren Pockets. Note: Includes pictures from Francis Ford Coppolas' Bram Stoker's Dracula.

Estonian
1990 *Graf Drakula: vampir.* [Tallinn, Estonia]: Valgus, 1990. 318 pp. Notes: Translation of: Dracula.

Finnish
1952 *Kammoittava Kreivi (Drakula).* Trans. by Rist Kalliomaa. Hameenlinna: Ed. Nide, 1952. 335 pp. hb. boards.

1977 *Dracula.* Trans. by Jarkko Laine. Helsinki: Ed. Otava, 1977. 415 pp.

1992 *Dracula.* Trans. by Jarkko Laine. Helsinki: Ed. Otava, 1992. 415 pp. hb. boards. Cover: Dracula with top hat.

Flemish

1974 *Dracula.* Trans. by Michael Grayn. Kapelle-Anvers, Belgium: Beckers, 1974. 341 pp.

Dracula. Trans. by Charles Robert. Kalmthout-Antwerpen [Kapelle-Anvers]: Beckers, 1974. 397 pp.

Flemish juvenile
1990 Adapted by Ataide Braz. Anvers (Antwerpen): Loempia, 1990. 47 pp.

French
The first translation of Dracula after World War I was the 1920 translation by Eve and Lucie Paul-Marguerite. It was translated on several occasions over the next half century and has continued to appear to the present time. The second translation, by Lucienne Molitor, first published in Belgium, appeared in 1963, and has been reprinted the most times. A newer translation, by Jacque Finné, was published in 1979. The first Swiss edition in French (Molitor translation) appeared in 1968 and the first French Canadian edition in 1976.

1920 *Dracula, l'homme de la nuit.* Trans. by Eve and Lucie Paul-Marguerite. Paris: L'Édition française illustrée, 1920. 262 pp.

Dracula, l'homme de la nuit. Trans. by Eve and Lucie Paul-Marguerite. Paris: Éditions G. Cres, 1920. Sereis: Collection littéraire des romans éstrangers. Reprinted 1921.

1932 *Dracula par Drahus Steker.* Trans. by Eve and Lucie Paul-Marguerite. Paris: Jules Tallandier, 1932. Series: Les Drames du coeur. Note: Includes stills from the Lugosi movie.

BIBLIOGRAPHICAL AFTERWORD 147

1946 *Dracula.* Trans. by Eve and Lucie Paul-Marguerite. Paris: Éditions des Quatres-Vents, 1946. 343 pp. Series: Les Maîtres du fantastique, dirigée par Henri Parisot.

1963 *Dracula.* Trans. by Lucienne Molitor. Verviers, Belgium: Gérard, 1963. 569 pp. pb. Series: Marabout Géant, no. 182. Introduction by Tony Faive.

Dracula. Trans. by Eve and Lucie Paul-Marguerite. Paris: Éditions le Terrain Vague, 1963. 172 pp. pb. Cover: Picture of Bela Lugosi. Note: This edition appeared as nos. 4-5 of Midi-Minuit Fantastique (January 1963). Texts also includes additional material including "L'auteur de Dracula" by Tony Faive; "Dracula au Cinema" by Jean-Claude Romer, a letter from Christopher Lee, and a bibliography prepared by Tony Faive and Jean-Claude Romer.

1967 *Dracula.* Paris: Éditions Baudelaire, 1967. 600 pp. Series: Livre Club.

Dracula. Trans. by Lucienne Molitor. Paris: Opta, 1968. 440 pp.

1968 *Dracula.* Trans. by Lucienne Molitor. Geneva: Edito-Service, 1968. Note: Preface and bibliography by Gilbert Sigaux.

1969 *Dracula.* Trans. by Lucienne Molitor. Paris: Cercle du Bibliophile, 1969.

1971 *Dracula.* Adaptation by Jean Arbuleau. Geneva-Petit-Lancy: Éditions Crémille/Paris: Éditions de l'Erable, 1971. 343 pp. Series: Chefs de oeuvre du mystère du fantastique. Abridged edition?

Mr. Bram Stoker
The well-known novelist and literary adviser to Sir Henry Irving, whose latest novel, "The Man," has just been published by Messrs. Heinemann

Photograph of Bram Stoker from The Bystander *(October 1905): 37.*

BIBLIOGRAPHICAL AFTERWORD 149

1975 *Dracula (le Chef d'oeuvre de l'épouvante).* Trans. by Lucienne Molitor. Verviers, Belgium: Éditions Marabout, no. 12, 1975. 507 pp. pb. Introduction by Tony Faivre. Reprinted: 1976, 1977.

1976 *Dracula.* Montreal: Éditions Heritage, 1976. 61 pp. Series: Classiques illustres Heritage. Note: Sur la couverture: Classiques en bandes illustrees.

1978 *Dracula.* Geneva: Éditions Fermi, 1978. 334 pp. Series: Les Cents Livres.

1979 *Dracula.* Trans. by Jacques Finné. Paris: Librarie de Champs-Elysees, 1979. 504 pp. pb. Series: Le Masque Fantastique, no. 17, second series. Introduction by Jacques Finne.

1980 *Dracula.* Trans. by Lucienne Molitor. Verviers, Belgium: Éditions Marabout, 1980. 506 pp. Series: Bibliothèque Marabout, 182.

1984 *Dracula.* Trans. by Lucienne Molitor. Verviers, Belgium: Éditions Marabout, 1984. 507 pp. Series: Bibliothèque Marabout, 182. Note: Preface by Tony Faive.

1987 *Dracula.* Trans. by Lucienne Molitor. Verviers, Belgium: Éditions Marabout, No. 12, January 1987. 507 pp. pb. Cover by Ph. Bertet.

1989 *Les Évadés des ténèbres.* Paris: Robert Laffont, 1989. 1139 pp. Note: Collected fiction with texts by Mary Shelley, Ann Radcliffe, Gustav Meyrink, Joseph Sheridan Le Fanu, and Dracula.

1992 *Dracula.* Trans. by Lucienne Molitor. Verviers, Belgium: Éditions Marabout, [1992]. 507 pp. pb. Introduction by Tony Faivre. Cover: Picture of Dracula (Gary Oldman) with Mina (Winona Ryder). Note: Edition published on the occasion of Francis Ford Coppola Film, Bram Stoker's Dracula.

Dracula. Trans. by Lucienne Molitor. Paris: France-Loisirs, 1992. 536 pp. pb. Introduction by Tony Faivre. Picture on cover of Gary Oldman as Dracula. Reprinted: 1993. Note: Reprint of Marabout edition. Edition published on the occasion of Francis Ford Coppola Film, Bram Stoker's Dracula.

Dracula. Trans. by Jacques Finné. Paris: Presses Pocket, 1992. 573 pp. pb. Cover: Dracula (Gary Oldman) embracing Mina (Winona Ryder). no. 4669. Note: Edition published on the occasion of Francis Ford Coppola Film, Bram Stoker's Dracula. Includes text of "Dracula's Guest" and a Dracula filmography.

1993 *Dracula.* Trans. by Lucienne Molitor. Verviers, Belgium: Éditions Marabout, [1992]. 507 pp. pb. No. 12 Introduction by Tony Faivre. Cover: Picture of Dracula (Gary Oldman) with Mina (Winona Ryder) with Dracula gargoyle. Note: Edition published on the occasion of Francis Ford Coppola Film, Bram Stoker's Dracula.

Dracula. Trans. by Lucienne Molitor. Paris: J'ai Lu, 1993. 506 pp. Series: Epouvante 3402. Cover: By Terry Oakes (Schlück). Note: Includes bibliography by Barbara Sadoul.

BIBLIOGRAPHICAL AFTERWORD 151

Dracula. Paris: France-Loisirs, (536) pp. hb. dj. Une édition du Club France. Introduction by Tony Faivre. Cover: Picture from Francis Ford Coppola's Bram Stoker's Dracula. Note: Reprinted from Marabout edition.

1994 *Dracula*. Trans. by Lucienne Molitor. Verviers, Belgium: Éditions Marabout, [1992]. 507 pp. pb. Series: Marabout Savoirs #9000. Introduction by Tony Faivre. Cover: Picture of Dracula (Gary Oldman) with Mina (Winona Ryder) with Dracula gargoyle. Note: Edition published on the occasion of Francis Ford Coppola Film, Bram Stoker's Dracula.

1996 *Dracula*. Trans. by Lucienne Molitor. Paris: J'ai Lu, 1996. 506 pp. pb. Series: Epouvante 3402. Cover: By Frank Frazetta. Note: Includes bibliography by Barbara Sadoul.

1997 *Dracula*. Tran by Lucienne Molitor. Arles: Babel, 1997. 603 pp. pb. Series Babel #268. Cover: John White Alexander, Isabel et le pot de basilic.

Vampires: Dracula et les Siens. Paris: Omnibus, 1997. 1263 pp. tp. Introduction by Roger Bozetto & Jean Marigny. Note: Omnibus edition that incules Dracula and other vampire novels and short stores.

Dracula. Genève: Éditions Famot, n.d. 340 pp. hb. Illus.: Claude Selva. Series: Collection les Chefs-d'Œuvre du Mystère et du Fantastique. Note: Private edition for subscribers only

French Adaptation
1979 *Dracula*. Adapted by Laurent Brault. St. Lambert, PQ: Éditions Herutage, 1979. 61 pp.

1988 *Dracula.* Adapted from text of Lucienne Molitor. Paris: Hachette, 1988. Series: Bibliothèque.

1998 *Dracula.* Milan: La Spiga Languages, 1998. 31 pp. pb. Series: Premières Lectures. Cover: Dracula with moon in background.

French Graphic Arts Adaptations
1981 *Dracula.* Trans. by G. Robert McConnel of text by Naunerle C. Farr. Montreal: Éditions Aquila, 1981. 64 pp. Note: Graphic art by Nestor Redondo. French Canadian reprint of Pendulum Press edition of 1973.

1993 Thomas, Roy, Mike Mignola, & John Nyberg, adapted by. Bram Stoker's Dracula. Grenoble: Collection Graphic U. S., 1993. 120 pp. tp. Graphic art version. Combines the four issues of the Topps' Bram Stoker's Dracula miniseries.

Gaelic
1933 *Dracula.* Trans. by Sean O. Cuirrin. Dublin: Oifig Diolta Foillseachain Railtaisin, 1933. 450 pp.

German
The 1908 edition of *Dracula* published in Leipzig is one of but two non-English editions published during Bram Stoker's lifetime.

1908 *Dracula.* Trans. by Heinz Widtmann. Leipzig: Max Altmann, 1908. 554 pp.

1967 *Dracula, ein Vampirroman.* Trans. by Stasi Kull [pseudonym of A. C. Artman]. Munich: Carl Hansen Verlag, 1967. 522 pp. hb.

BIBLIOGRAPHICAL AFTERWORD 153

Dracula. Trans. of Stasi Kull. Zurich: Buchclub Ex Libros, 1967. 522 pp. Note: Book club reprint of original Hansen edition.

Dracula. Trans. by Karl Bruno Leder. Geneva/Hamburg: Kossodo Verlag, 1967. 415 pp. Series: Horrro Mundi.

1968 *Dracula, ein Vampirroman.* Trans. By Stasi Kull. Munich: Deutscher Taschenbuch Verlag, 1968. 499 pp. pb. Reprinted: 1969, 1979, 1981.

Dracula. Trans. by Wulf H. Bergner. Olten: Fackelverlag, 1968. 404 pp.

1969 *Dracula, ein Vampirroman.* Trans. of Stasi Kull. Munich: Deutscher Taschenbuch Verlag, 1969. 499 pp. pb. DT 516.

1970 *Dracula.* Trans. of Stasi Kull. Zurich: Neue Schweizer Bibliothek, 1970. 523 pp.

1976 *Dracula.* Trans. of Stasi Kull. Stuttgart/Hambiurg/Munich: Deutscher Bücherbund, 1976. 522 pp. Note: Club edition reserved for members.

1979 *Dracula, ein Vampirroman.* Trans. of Stasi Kull. Munich: Taschenbuch Verlag, 1979. 429 pp.

Dracula. Trans. by Karl Bruno Leder. Stuttgart: Europäische Bildungsgemeinschaft, 1979. 414 pp. Note: Special edition for member of the Europäische Bildungsgemeinschaft, a cultural association.

Dracula. Trans. by Wulf H. Bergner. Munich: Heyne Verlag, 1979. 299 pp. Series: Heyne-Buch, 526. Reprinted: 1988, 1990, 1991. Abridged edition?

1981 *Dracula.* Trans. of Stasi Kull. Munich: Schneider Verlag, 1981. 155 pp. Series: Schneider Taschen-bücher, 282.

Dracula, ein Vampirroman. Trans. of Stasi Kull. Munich: Taschenbuch Verlag, 1981. 429 pp.

1988 *Dracula.* Trans. by Wulf H. Bergner. Munich: Heyne Verlag, 1988. 299 pp. Series: Heyne-Buch, 526.

Dracula. Trans. by Karl Bruno Leder. Frankfurt-am-Main: Insel-Verlag, 1988. 540 pp. pb. Series: Insel-Taschenbuch, 1806. Reprinted: 1991, 1995

1989 *Dracula, ein Vampirroman.* Trans by ? Berlin: Das Nue Berlin, 1989. 405 pp. hb. Afterword by Helge Martini. Illustrated by Volker Pfüller. Reprinted 1990.

Dracula. Trans of Karl Bruno Leder. Gutersloh: Bertelsmann-Club, 1989. 414 pp. Reprinted 1993. Note: Special edition for members of the Bertelsmann Club reprinted with authorization of Kossodo Verlag.

1990 *Dracula.* Trans. by Wulf H. Bergner. Munich: Heyne Verlag, 1990. 299 pp. Series: Heyne-Bücher, 01; Heyne Allgemeine Reihe, 526.

Dracula. Trans. by Wulf H. Bergner. Rastatt: Moewig, 1990. (300) pp. Series: Moewig, 2721. Reprint of Heyne verlag edition.

Dracula. Trans. by ? Berlin: Kupfergraben, 1990. (405) pp. Authorized reprint of Neue Berklin edition. Ed. by Helge Martini.

BIBLIOGRAPHICAL AFTERWORD 155

1991 *Dracula.* Trans. by Wulf H. Bergner. Munich: Heyne Verlag, 1991. 299 pp. Series: Heyne-Bücher, 01; Heyne Allgemeine Reihe, 526.

Dracula. Trans. by Karl Bruno Leder. Frankfurt-am-Main: Insel-Verlag, 1991. 540 pp. Series: Insel-Taschenbuch, 1806.

1992 *Dracula, ein Vampirroman.* Trans. by Stasi Kull. Vienna/Munich: Hansen Verlag, 1992. 522 pp. hb. boards. Cover: Black with red lettering and dropps of blood.

1993 *Dracula.* Trans. of Stasi Kull. Munich: Goldman Verlag, 1993. 522 pp. pb. Series: Goldman, 42076.

Dracula, ein Vampirroman. Trans. by Stasi Kull. Frankfort/Vienna: Büchergilde Gutenberg, 1993. 522 pp. Note: Book club edition.

Dracula. Trans. by Karl Bruno Leder. Frankfurt-am-Main: Insel-Verlag, 1993. 540 pp. Series: Insel-Taschenbuch, 1806.

Dracula. Trans. by Bernhard Willms. Bergisch Gladbach, Bastei-Verlag, Luebbe, 1993. 539 pp. pb Series: Bastei-Lübbe-Taschenbuchprogramm, Band 13449.

Dracula. Trans of Karl Bruno Leder. Gutersloh: Bertelsmann-Club, 1993. 414 pp. Note: Reprint of special edition for members of the Bertelsmann Club reprinted with authorization of Kossodo Verlag

Dracula. Trans. by Wulf H. Bergner. Munich: Heyne Verlag, 1990. 334 pp. pb. Series: Heyne-Bücher, 01; Heyne Allgemeine Reihe, 526. Cover: Frank Langella as Dracula.

Dracula. Trans. by Wulf H. Bergner. Berlin: Moewig bei Ullstein, 1993. 300 pp. Cover: Dracula (Gary Oldman) with Mina (Winona Ryder). Note: Reprint authorized by Heyne Verlag.

1994 *Dracula.* Trans. by Ulrike Bishoff. Köln: Könemann, 1994. 492 pp. hb. Reprinted 1995.

Dracula. Trans. by Stasi Kull. Vienna/Munich: Hansen Verlag, 1994. 522 pp.

1995 *Dracula.* Trans. by Bernhard Willms. Bergisch Gladbach, Bastei-Verlag, Luebbe, 1993. 539 pp. pb Series: Bastei-Lübbe-Taschenbuchprogramm, Band 13449. Cover: Dracula in front of castle anf full moon. Repint on occasion of Francis Ford Coppola's Dracula.

Dracula. Text revised by Franz Schrapfeneder. Vienna: Tosa-Verlag, 1995. 297 pp.

Dracula. Trans. by Karl Bruno Leder. Frankfurt-am-Main: Insel-Verlag, 1995. 540 pp. Series: Insel-Taschenbuch, 1806.

1998 *Dracula, ein Vampirroman.* Trans by ? Berlin: Ullstein Buchverlage, 1998. 473 pp. pb. Cover: stained-glass window. Taschenbuch 24317.

2000 *Dracula, ein Vampirroman.* Trans. by Stasi Kull. München: Deutscher Tashenbuch Verlag, 1992, 2000. 549 pp. pb. Cover: Cover: Dracula's Castle. Black backgrounf with red letters.

German Graphic Art Adaptations
1993 Thomas, Roy, Mike Mignola, & John Nyberg, adapted by. *Bram Stoker's Dracula.* Stuttgart: Feest USA, 1993. 120

BIBLIOGRAPHICAL AFTERWORD 157

pp. tp. Graphic art version. Combines the four issues of the Topps' Bram Stoker's Dracula mini-series.

Greek
1959 *Drakoulas: o vrykolakas tion Karpathieon.* Trans. by ? Athènes: Darema, 1959. 400 pp.

Hebrew
1984 *Drakulah.* Yerushalayim: Elisar, 1984. 396 pp. Alt. title: Dracula. Hebrew.

Hungarian
1985 *Drakula grof Valogatott remtettei.* Trans. by Bartos Tibor. Budapest: Arkadia, 1985. 290 pp. pb. Cover: Bela Lugosi as Dracula.

1990 *Drakula: angol regeny.* Trans. by Tar Ferencz. 1990?

1993 *Drakula.* Trans. by Both Vilmos. Ed. Intercom, Debrecen Alföldi NY, 1993. ?

1995 *Drakula, a Vampyr.* Tran. by Bartos Tibor. Budapest: Meranyi, 1995. 253 pp. Introduction by Stephen King.

Icelandic
This initial translation of Dracula was the first one made during Stoker's life. It is an abridged edition translated by Valdimar Asmundsson for the publisher Nokkrir Prentarar. It is of primary interest as Stoker yeilded to Prentarar's request that he write a new preface for it. An English translation of that preface first appeared in *The Bram Stoker Society Journal* 5 (1993): 7-8.

1901 *Makt Myrkanna* [*Power of Darkness*]. Trans. by Valdimar Ásmundsson. Reykjavík: Prentud í Félagsprentsmidjunni, 1901. 220 pp. pb. Preface by Bram Stoker.

Indonesian

1993 *Drakula.* Trans. by ? Jakarta: Gramedia Pustaka Utama, 1993. 2 vols.

Italian

1922 *Dracula. L'uomo della notte.* Abridged edition. Trans. by A. Nessi. Milano: Sonzogno, 1922.

1945 *Dracula.* Trans. by Riccardo Selvi [the name of the translator is not indicated]. Milano: Fratelli Bocca, 1945.

1952 *Dracula.* Trans. by Riccardo Selvi [second edition, with a different cover; the name of the translator is indicated]. Milano: Fratelli Bocca, 1952.

1959 *Dracula il vampiro.* Trans by Adriana Pellegrini. Milano: Longanesi, 1959.

1966 *Dracula, il principe delle tenebre.* Trans. by Remo Fedi. Milano: Sugar, 1966. 270 pp. hb. Note: Blue dust jacket with picture of Christopher Lee as Dracula.

Dracula, il vampiro. Trans. by Adriana Pellegrini. Milano: Longanesi & Co., 1966. 323 pp. pb. Series: Il Libri Pocket.

1972 *Dracula, il principe delle tenebre.* Trans. by Remo Fedi. Milano: Club degli Editori, 1972. 269 pp. Series: Il laccio nero, 2.

1975 *Dracula.* Milano: Longanesi, 1975. 299 pp.

1976 *Dracula.* Milano: I grandi libri di Gente, 1976. 322 pp. pb. Red cover, no picture.

BIBLIOGRAPHICAL AFTERWORD 159

1979 *Dracula.* Trans. by Francesco Saba Sardi. Milano: A. Mondadori Editore, 1979. 436 pp. tp. Introduction by Francesco Saba Sardi. Cover: Dracula with black border. Published on occasion of Universal's Dracula starring Frank Langella. Yellow banner advertising film. Undated reprints. Cover: Ruins of Castle Dracula. Reprinted: 1994. Cover: Black background. Dracula in red running as if blood.

Dracula. Trans. by Adriana Pellegrini. Milano: Longanesi & Co., 1979. 287 pp. tp. Cover: Poster of Nosferatu movie.

Dracula. Milano: Sugar Co. Edizioni, 1979. 347 pp.

1987 *Conte Dracula.* Graphic art by Crepax. Milano: Rizzoli, 1987. 142 pp. pb. Black and white comic version.

1992 *Dracula.* Trans. by Adriana Pellegrini. Milano: Teadue, 1992. 323 pp. pb. Licensed from Longanesi. Reprinted: February 1993.

1993 *Dracula.* Trans. by Francesco Saba Sardi. Milano: A. Mondadori, 1993. 435 pp.

Dracula. Rome: Grandi tascabili economici Newton, 1993. 313 pp. Series: Classici del mistero. Ed. by Paola Faini. Introduction by Riccardo Reim. Cover: "Man and Woman Contemplating the Moor" by Caspar David Freidrich.

Dracula. Trans. by Adriana Pellegrini. Milano: Teadue, 1993. 323 pp. pb. Cover: Drawing of female fleeing a horror.

Dracula. Trans. by Rosanna Pelà. Biblioteca Universale Rizzoli, 1993. 507 pp. pb. Postscript by Carlo Pagetti. Cover: Gary Oldman as Dracula from Bram Stoker's Dracula.

Dracula. Trans. by Marina De Luca and John Irving. Torino/Firenze: Pluriverso, 1993. 502 pp. tp. Cover: Noferatu in shadow. Blue background.

1994 *Dracula.* Trans. by Rosanna Pelà. Biblioteca Universale Rizzoli, 1994. 507 pp. pb. Postscript by Carlo Pagetti. Cover: Gary Oldman as Dracula from Bram Stoker's Dracula. S144.

1996 *Dracula.* Trans. by Paola Faini. Rome: Biblioteca Economica Newton, 1996. 333 pp. tp. Series: Classici Ben #82. Introduction by Riccardo Reim. Dracula filmography, pp.314-331. Cover: "Man and Woman Contemplating the Moor" by Caspar David Freidrich.

Dracula. Trans. by Rosanna Pelà. Biblioteca Universale Rizzoli, 1996. 507 pp. pb. Postscript by Carlo Pagetti. Cover: Gary Oldman as Dracula from Bram Stoker's Dracula. S144.

I grandi romanzi dell'orrore. Trans. by Paolo Faini. Milano: Grandi Tascabili Economici Newton, 1996. 922 pp. tp. Series: I Mammut. Cover: Maxfield Parish's Snow White. Notes: Combined edition of *Dracula, Frankenstein,* and *The Strange Case of Dr. Jekyll and Mr. Hyde* with *Vathek* by W. Beckford, *La Casa sull'Abisso* by Hodgson, *The Golem* by Meyrink, *Stripe du Lupe* by Munn, and *Le Montagne dlla Follia* by Lovecraft.

BIBLIOGRAPHICAL AFTERWORD 161

2001 *Dracula.* Milano: BUR/Rizzoli Libri, 2001. 504 pp. tp. First edition. Trans. by Rosanna Pelà. Preface by Vittorino Andreoli. Reprint of 1993 Rizzoli edition.

2002 *Dracula.* Milano: BUR/Rizzoli Libri, 2002. 504 pp. tp. Second edition. Trans. by Rosanna Pelà. Preface by Vittorino Andreoli. Reprint of 1993 Rizzoli edition.

Italian Adaptations

Fletcher-Watson, adaptation by Jo. *Dracula.* Illus. by Tutor Humphries. Novaro: Instituto Geografico De Agostini, 1998 64 pp. hb. Series: In pimo piano Classici.

Italian Graphic Arts Adaptations

Crepax, Guido. "Conte Dracula." 12 parts. *Corto Maltese* I, 1 (October 1983)—II, 9 (September 1984).

———. *Conte Dracula.* Milano: Milano Libri, 1989. 142 pp. pb. large format.

———. *Conte Dracula.* N.p.: Hobby and Work, 1998. 142 pp. hb. boards. Red lettering on black background. Slip case cover: Dracula biting nude female. Large format.

Thomas, Roy, Mike Mignola, & John Nyberg, adapted by. *Bram Stoker's Dracula.* Star Comics, 1993. 120 pp. tp. Graphic art version. Combines the four issues of the Topps' *Bram Stoker's Dracula* mini-series.

Japanese

199? *Dracula.* 559 pp. pb #502 01 780. All publication information is in the Japanese language.

Dracula. 559 pp. pb. #502 01 880. All publication information is in the Japanese language.

Korean

1992 Durakyulla: Buraem Sutoko changpyon sosol. 2 vols. Chopan, Soul Tukpyolsi: Yollin Chaekdul, 1992. Alt. title: Dracula. Korean.

1983 Huphyolgwi Turakyulla. Chungpan, Soul-si: Kyerim Chulpansa, 1983. 192 pp. Series: Sonyon sonyo yongwonhan segye ui myongjak mungo, 163. Notes: Translation of Dracula.

Lithuanian

1991 *Drakula*. Trans. by Kestulis Sidiskis. Vilnius: Amzius, 1991. 286 pp.

1992 *Drakula*. Trans. by Kestulis Sidiskis. Vilnius: Amzius, 1992. 286 pp.

Malaysian

1990 *Dracula*. Trans. by Yeap Johari Yoakob. Petating Jaya: ed. Penerbit Fajar Bakti, 1990. 314 pp.

Norwegian

1974 *Dracula*. Trans. by Bjorn Carling. Oslo: Gyldendal, 1974. 395 pp.

1980 *Dracula*. Trans. by Bjorn Carling. Stabekk: Den Norse Bokkluben, 1980. 470 pp. Book club edition. Preface by Bing Bringswoord.

1993 *Dracula*. Trans. by Bjorn Carling. Stabekk: Bokkluben Krim og Spenning, 1993. 435 pp.

Polish

1990 *Dracula*. Jelemia Gora: Civis Press, 1990. Note: Bound with Wampir by W. Polidori.

BIBLIOGRAPHICAL AFTERWORD 163

Portuguese
1972 *Dracula*. Lisbonne: Editorial Minerva, 1972. 271 pp. pb. Series: Minerva de bolso, 7. Cover: Dracula with tombstones. Reprint: 1975. Reprint: 1993. Cover: Dracula with tombs. White background.

1985 *Dracula*. Porto Alegre, Rio Grande do Sul, Brazil: L&PM, 1985. 462 pp.

Romanian
1990 *Dracula*. Trans. by Barbu Coculescu and Lleana Verza. Bucharest: Univers, 1990. 430 pp. hb. boards. Cover: Eagle, chalice and candlelabra. Introduction and notes by Barbu Coculescu and Lleana Verza.

1993 *Dracula*. Trans. by Barbu Coculescu and Lleana Verza. Bucharest: Univers, 1993. 428 pp. tp. Cover: Montage of pictures on red background. White lettering. Introduction and notes by Barbu Coculescu and Lleana Verza. Carries note that Dracula was first published in the United States in 1897 and first published in Great Britain by Rider in 1912.

Dracula. Trans. by Barbu Coculescu and Lleana Verza. Craiova: Tribuna, 1993. 391 pp. Edited by Valeriu Campeanu.

1997 *Dracula*. Trans. by Barbu Coculescu and Lleana Verza. Bucharesti: Editura "Tess express," 1997. 179 pp. pb. Cover: Drawing of fanged Dracula. Abridged edition.

Russian
1993 *Dracula*. Trans by A. Birgera. Moscou: ed. Renessans, 1993. 431 pp. Series: Mir Mistiki.

Dracula. Saint Petersburg: Aebuka, 2000. hp. 478 pp. Cover: Victim of cholera buried prematurely in coffin, painting by Antoine-Joseph Wiertz (same as 1992 Signet edition). Publishing information is in the Cyrillic alphabet.

Spanish

Dracula has been translated into Spanish more times than any other language. At least seven translations have been discovered, the first being in 1966.

1966 *Dracula*. Madrid: Molino, 1966.

1973 *Dracula*. Trans. by Francisco Torres Oliver ? Barcelona, Spain: Bruguera, 1973. 555 pp.

1979 *Dracula*. Barcelona: Producciones Editoriales, 1979. 391 pp.

1980 *Dracula*. Mexico: Editorial V Siglos, 1980. 265 pp.

Dracula. Trans. by Mario Montalban. Barcelona, Spain: Esplugas de Llobregat, Plaza & Janes, 1980, 457 pp.

1981 *Dracula*. Trans. by Francisco Torres Oliver. Barcelona, Spain: Bruguera, 1981. 511 pp. Series: Libro amigo.

Dracula. Mexico: Picazo, 1981. 415 pp.

1984 *Dracula*. Mexico, D.F.: Origen-Planeta, 1984. 511 pp. Series: Best sellers, no. 21.

Dracula. Barcelona, Spain: Editors S.A., 1984. 415 pp.

Dracula. Trans. by Fernando Trôas. Madrid: Fasciculo Planeta, 1984. 2 vols.

BIBLIOGRAPHICAL AFTERWORD 165

Dracula. Trans. by Sylvia Aymerich. Barcelona: Laertes, 1984. 465 pp. Series: El Libros de Glauco, 8. Reprinted: 1989.

Dracula. Trans. by Flora Casas. Madrid, Spain: E. G. Anaya, 1984/1987. 398 pp. hb. boards. Illus. by Matilde Garcá-Monzón. Afterword by Noel Zanquín Subirats.Series: Tus libros intriga, 39. 2nd edition, 1987. 3rd edition, 1989. 4th edition, 1991. 5th edition, 1992. 6th edition, 1993. 7th edition, 1994. 8th edition, 1995. Cover: Bat flying over London.

Biblioteca del Terror: Dracula I. Barcelona: Ediciones Forum, 1984. 87 pp. pb. Cover: Christopher Lee and Bela Lugosi.

1985 *Dracula.* Barcelona, Spain: Editors, 1985. 415 pp.

Dracula. Trans. by Francisco Torres Oliver. Barcelona: Bruguera, 1985. 511 pp. Series: Libro amigo, no. 878.

1986 *Dracula.* Trans. by Manio Montalban. Barcelona: Esplugues de Llobregat, Plaza & Janos, 1986. 457 pp. Series: El Ave Fanix, 79. Reprinted: 1990.

1989 *Dracula.* Barcelona, Spain: Montesinos, 1989. 379 pp.

Dracula. Trans. by Sylvia Aymerich. Barcelona: Laertes, 1989. 465 pp. Series: L'arco, 8.

1990 *Dracula.* Trans. by Manio Montalban. Barcelona: Esplugues de Llobregat, Plaza & Janos, 1990. 457 pp. Series: El Ave Fanix Narrativia, 79.

1992 *Dracula.* Trans. by Manio Montalban. Barcelona: Esplugues de Llobregat, Plaza & Janos, 1990. 457 pp. Series: Los jet de Plaza et Janos, 200.

Drácula. Barcelona, Spain: Ultramar Editores, December 1992. 398 pp. hb. Reprinted: 1993.

Dracula. Trans. by Francisco Torres Oliver. Barcelona: Editiones B, 1992. 490 pp.

1993 *Dracula.* Madrid, Spain: Ediciones Gaviota, 1993. 325 pp. Notes: "Version integra"—Jacket. Undated reprint: hb. boards. Cover: hand coming out of coffin.

Dracula. Trans. by Juan Antonio Molina Foix. Madrid: Catedra, 1993. 630 pp. Series: Letras universales, 195. Introduction by Juan Antonio Molina Foix. Bibliography. Cover: Gary Oldman as Dracula.

Dracula: la novela original. Trans. by Manio Montalban. Barcelona, Plaza & Janes, 1993. 457 pp.

Drácula. Barcelona, Spain: Ultramar Editores, January 1993. 398 pp. hb. Dust jacket: Christopher Lee as Dracula, tomb of Vlad Tepes.

Dracula. Madrid: Mateos, 1993. 391 pp.

Dracula. Trans. by Flora Casas. Barcelona: Altaya, 1993, 365 pp. Series: Biblioteca de adventuras y misterio, 6.

1994 *Dracula.* Trans. by Manio Montalban. Barcelona, Spain: Plaza & Janes Editores, 1994. 458 pp. pb. Cover: Gargoyle from Coppola's Bram Stokers' Dracula. 5th reprinting.

Dracula. Trans. by Francisco Torres Oliver. Barcelona: Montesinos, 1994. 397 pp. Series: Visio Tondali, 127, Classicos. Undated reprint. tp. Cover: woman with bite marks on neck.

Dracula. Madrid: Mateos, 1994. 351 pp. Series: Biblioteca DM. Novela.

1995 *Dracula.* Trans. by Manio Montalban. Barcelona: Orbis, 1995. 457 pp.

Dracula. Trans. by Francisco Torres Oliver. Barcelona: Editiones B, 1995. 512 pp. pb. Cover: youthful Dracula.

1997 *Dracula.* Trans. by Francisco Torres Oliver. Barcelona: Editiones B, 1995. 512 pp. pb. Cover: Gary Oldman and Winona Rider as Dracula and Mina.

1999 *Dracula.* Col. Portales, Mexico: Editorial Época, 1999. 492 pp. tp. Cover: Nosferatu statue, white background. Series: Siempre Claasicos.

2000 *Drácula.* Nicolás San Juan, Mexico: Grupo Editorial Tomo, 2000. 547 pp. tp. Cover: Dracula's face over Castle Bran.

Drácula. N.p.: Kovela Biblioteca DM, n.d.. 351 pp. tp. Cover Black background with bat and fangs.

Spanish Adaptation
1982 Trans. by Rodolfo Heller of text by Naunerle C. Farr. Madrid: Ediprint, 1982. 61 pp. Graphic art by Nestor Redondo. Note: Spanish reprint of Pendulum Press edition of 1973.

1984 Adapted by Fernando Fernandez. Barcelona: Toutain, 1984. 96 pp. Barcelona: Timun Mas, 1984. 38 p. Series: Dos una. Cover title: Dos una = Dracula.

1985 Trans by Steven Owen. London: Heineman/Madrid: Itaca, 1985. 77 pp. Note: Parallel English/Spanish texts.

Trans. by Flora Casas. Madrid: Cadice D. L., 1995. 367 pp. Series: Biblioteca Classicos Juveniels, 7.

Swedish

1965 *Dracula*. Trans. by Berit Skrogsberg. Stockholm: AWE\Geber, 1965. 399 pp. Reprint: Trans. by Berit Skrogsberg. Stockholm: AWE\Geber, 1979. 399 pp.

1980 *Dracula*. Trans. by Sam J. Lundwall. Hoganos (?): Bra Böcher/Klassika Deckare, 1980. 311 pp. hb. Dust jacket: Klaus Kinski as Noferatu.

1980 *Dracula*. Trans. by Sam J. Lundwall. Hoganas (?): ed. Wilken, 1993. 311 pp.

Swedish Adaptations

1973 *Dracula*

Thai

??? *Dracula*. Bangkok: ed. by Mei Sai, ?

Ukrainian

2002 *Dracula*. Lviv: Vydabnychy dim Panorama. tp. Trans. of Penguin/Godfrey Cave edition. Cover: Dracula's face with castle in background. Publishing information is in the Ukrainian alphabet.

NOTES

[1] Here is the first instance, among the reviews collected here, in which the reviewer associates *Dracula* with the werewolf legend. This may come as strange to modern-day readers and film-goers, who have grown accustomed to seeing Dracula and vampires transform into wolves on screen and in literature. However, this convention was to *fin de siècle* readers relatively unfamiliar— practically an innovation at the hands of Stoker. It is interesting to note that in European folklore, wolves were generally antagonistic to vampires, digging up their bodies from the ground and partially consuming them. This, in part, may have contributed to the idea that vampires, while in the grave, chewed on their own shrouds, and on themselves; fearful villagers who were unaware of the wolves, who generally foraged at night (a period during which villagers did not venture about), naturally assumed the vampire to be feeding on itself. See Paul Barber, *Vampire, Burial, and Death: Folklore and Reality* (New Haven, CT: Yale University Press, 2010 [1988]).

[2] The reviewer is here referring to the French Benedictine Antoine Augustin Calmet (1672–1757), author of the seminal treatise on vampirism *Dissertations sur les Apparitions des Anges, des Démons et des Esprits, et sur les Revenants et Vampires de Hongrie, de Bohême, de Moravie, et de Silésie* (Paris, 1746).

[3] This reviewer is among several who mistake the Dutch Professor for a German; Van Helsing hails from Amsterdam.

[4] This reviewer foretells one of several attributes—the contemporization of the vampire myth—that, in the reviews that follow and for many years to come, are by many commonly cited for *Dracula*'s enduring success.

5 A passage from the anonymously written vampire tale "The Mysterious Stranger: A Tale," published in *Chambers's Repository of Instructive and Amusing Facts* 8, no. 62 (London and Edinburgh: William and Robert Chambers, 1854): 1-32, offers insight into Stoker's "research" for *Dracula*:

> The ferocious [wolves] were but a few steps behind the travellers. Every now and then they retired, and set up a ferocious howl. The party had just arrived at the old oak before mentioned, and were about to turn into the path to the ruins [of the castle], when the animals, as though perceiving the risk they ran of losing their prey, came so near that a lance could easily have struck them. The knight and Franz faced sharply about, spurring their horses amidst the advancing crowds, when suddenly, from the shadow of the oak stepped forth a man, who in a few strides placed himself between the travellers and their pursuers. As far as one could see in the dusky light, the stranger was a man of a tall and well-built frame; he wore a sword by his side, and a broad-brimmed hat was on his head. If the party were astonished at his sudden appearance, they were still more so at what followed. As soon as the stranger appeared, the wolves gave over their pursuit, rumbled over each other, and set up a fearful howl. The stranger now raised his hand, appeared to wave it, and the wild animals crawled back into the thickets like a pack of beaten hounds.
>
> Without casting a glance at the travellers, who were too much overcome by astonishment to speak, the stranger went up the path which led to the castle, and soon disappeared beneath the gateway. (7)

THE MYSTERIOUS STRANGER.

TRANSLATED FROM THE GERMAN.

'To die?—to sleep!
Perchance to dream? Ay, there's the rub.'—*Hamlet.*

OREAS, that fearful north-west wind, which in the spring and autumn stirs up the lowest depths of the wild Adriatic, and is then so dangerous to vessels, was howling through the woods, and tossing the branches of the old knotty oaks in the Carpathian Mountains, when a party of five riders, who surrounded a litter drawn by a pair of mules, turned into a forest-path, which offered some protection from the April weather, and allowed the travellers in some degree to recover their breath. It was already evening, and bitterly cold; the snow fell every now and then in large flakes. A tall

No. 62.   1

Title page for the anonymously written "The Mysterious Stranger: A Tale" from Chambers's Repository of Instructive and Amusing Facts *8, no. 62 (William and Robert Chambers, 1854): 1.*

[6] With the possible exception of the 1899 first American edition of *Dracula*, unless these pipe-smoking reviewers are female, they have little to fear from Dracula, who generally takes female victims. As Nina Auerbach and David J. Skal point out in their Norton critical edition of Stoker's novel, *Dracula: Authoritative Text, Contexts, Reviews & Reactions, Dramatic and Film Variations, Criticism* (New York: W. W. Norton & Co., 1997), unlike the British edition(s), wherein at the end of chapter four (29 June) Jonathan hears the three vampire brides whispering outside his door and Dracula calling to them, "'Back, back, to your own place! Your time is not yet come. Wait. Have patience. Tomorrow night, to-morrow night is yours!'," in the 1899 American edition the last sentence reads, "'To-night is mine. To-morrow night is yours!'," thus insinuating Dracula's intention to feed on Jonathan (52). That Stoker excised this line "was understandable," note Auerbach and Skal, "for it leads to a different novel, one unpublishable in 1897 England; Stoker may have imagined that the America that produced his hero Walt Whitman would be more tolerant of men feeding on men" (52). I have found the same to be true of the American "Three Owls Edition" of *Dracula: A Mystery Story* (New York: W. R. Caldwell & Co., c.1918 [1897]) (51).

By 1931, however, Universal executive Carl Laemmle, Jr. would reinstitute Dracula's earlier, more conservative victimology, writing on an earlier draft (the Bromfield-Murphy script [September 8, 1930]) of *Dracula* (1931) in response to the Varna's (Demeter's) arrival to England: "'What happened to the crew? Explain in dialog? How? . . . Dracula should only go for women not men" (56). See Philip J. Riley's *Dracula: The Original 1931 Shooting Script* (Atlantic City and Hollywood: MagicImage Film Books, 1990).

[7] Here, too, is another commonly cited distinction of Stoker's novel that offers valuable insight into the novel's success.

[8] David Pirie remarks in his seminal work *The Vampire Cinema* (New York: Crescent Books, 1977) that "If there is one magic ingredient of the vampire genre in literature or in the cinema, one

that sometimes even supersedes the vampire himself, it is the *landscape* he inhabits" (41). He adds, "The vampire may be the active agent of terror, but the passive agent is the landscape" and it "must be utilised to supply a quality of remoteness without which the vampire might become completely mundane"; for, the vampire is after all, "in narrative form, a Gothic creation, and consequently [its] relation with Gothic landscape is an intimate one" (41).

9 Here, again, we see praised Stoker's juxtaposition of the ordinary and everyday with the fantastic.

10 For a thorough elucidation of this topic, see Robert Eighteen-Bisang and Elizabeth Miller's *Bram Stoker's Notes for Dracula: A Facsimile Edition* (Jefferson, NC: McFarland, 2008).

11 This reviewer agrees with Pirie's assessment regarding Gothic geography and exotic locales yet departs from the other reviewers' consensus about the effectiveness of Stoker's modernization of this convention, or what may be called the "urban Gothic."

12 The "reality" and possibility of Stoker's fantastic narrative are on this occasion derived from the novel's epistolary structure.

13 Readers of the present volume will recognize in this phrase a precursor to HBO's *True Blood* (TV, 2008-).

14 The reviewer here alludes to the infamous "Jack the Ripper" case, which Stoker, too, discusses in the preface to the abridged Icelandic edition of *Dracula* in 1901. See Robert Eighteen-Bisang and J. Gordon Melton's "*Dracula* in Print: A Checklist," in *Dracula in Visual Media: Film, Television, Comic Book and Electronic Game Appearances*, by John Edgar Browning and Caroline Joan (Kay) Picart (Jefferson, NC: McFarland, 2012), 268.

15 Later works by scholars and Gothicists treating the Dracula/Wanderer discourse include, among others: Howard L. Malchow's *Gothic Images of Race in Nineteenth-Century Britain* (Palo Alto, CA: Stanford University Press, 1996); Judith Halberstam's *Skin Shows: Gothic Horror and the Technology of Monsters* (Durham, NC: Duke University Press, 1995); and Ôrît

Kamîr's *Every Breath You Take: Stalking Narratives and the Law* (Ann Arbor, MI: University of Michigan Press, 2001).

[16] I have placed Stoddard's questions in italics for ease of differentiation from Stoker's answers.

[17] Styria is, in fact, where Stoker originally laid his tale. See Eighteen-Bisang and Miller's *Bram Stoker's Notes for Dracula*.

[18] See "Appendix IV: Bram Stoker's Nonfiction Sources for *Dracula*," in Eighteen-Bisang and Miller's *Bram Stoker's Notes for Dracula* (304-305).

[19] Be it Russian or Transylvanian, the point here is "Eastern" (i.e. exotic, thus strange and peculiar). An especially lengthy treatment of this subject may be found in Jimme E. Cain, Jr.'s *Bram Stoker and Russophobia: Evidence of the British Fear of Russia in Dracula and The Lady of the Shroud* (Jefferson, NC: McFarland, 2006).

[20] This is quite a compliment to an author whose book saw only "mixed" reviews.

[21] The reviewer here means, of course, "Dr. [S]eward's diary."

[22] The original letter is located at the Harry Ransom Humanities Research Center, University of Texas, at Austin; quoted in Elizabeth Miller, ed., *Bram Stoker's Dracula: A Documentary Journey into Vampire Country and the Dracula Phenomenon* (New York: Pegasus Books, 2009).

[23] The reviewer means here "b[l]oofer lady."

[24] According to Robert Gavora, Fine and Rare Books, Charles Cullom Parker is noted as Los Angeles's first bookstore owner and indeed one of the founders of "Downtown's Bookstore Row." See "Adobe Days," *Robert Gavora, Fine and Rare Books*, accessed November 12, 2011, http://www.robertgavora.com/shop/gavora/31377.html.

[25] The Bram Stoker Estate, David J. Skal, and I have ascertained independently at least three separate newspapers printed between 1899-1921 in which *Dracula* appeared in serial form, in addition to the *Argosy* magazine printing of 1926.

[26] This reviewer has obviously misread or been misinformed

about the novel, as Dracula is not, in the end, beheaded nor does he suffer a stake through the heart.

[27] This reviewer elegantly captures the skill and realism with which Stoker infuses his novel.

[28] Though much as this review, at surface level, denounces Stoker's *Dracula*, it achieved, in all likelihood, an effect not intended by the reviewer (or, perhaps intended, by means of sarcastic device), by affirming the novel's morbidity for readers who, after reading the review, probably did anything but avoid Stoker's novel.

[29] I have been unable to locate any evidence that *Dracula* ever appeared in serial form in England. It is possible here the reviewer meant America.

[30] The reviewer is referring here to Bram Stoker.

[31] This reviewer's words are prophetic.

[32] On April 23, 1912, *The New York Times* published the following obituary:

> As the fidus Achates of HENRY IRVING, and later as his Boswell, BRAM STOKER, who just died in London, gained international fame. He had no special vocation for theatrical management, and until he became IRVING's business manager and "personal representative," in 1878, he had had little if any theatrical training. He was a tall, blonde Irishman, who had been well educated in Dublin, and had filled small positions in the civil service. But he had theatrical inclinations, and had once applied to MR. and MRS. KENDAL for employment as business manager. They felt afterward that they had reason to regret their refusal to employ him.
>
> Yet he might never have had the success in that field with another employer than IRVING. The great actor and his friend had long been friends. IRVING placed implicit confidence in STOKER'S

judgment and business sense, while STOKER looked upon IRVING as the only supremely great man in the world. Their relationship lasted from the beginning of IRVING'S career as manager of the London Lyceum until his death. STOKER relieved Irving of every possible care, was the active host at the famous supper parties, stood between IRVING and the crowd of theatrical aspirants and would-be playwrights. He paid the bills and arranged all the details of transportation. He was never tired, and never depressed. He remembered the faces and names of all he ever met, or, if he did not, he had the skill to make others believe he did. Undoubtedly much of IRVING'S success was due to him.

For the rest, he wrote fluently and was eagerly interested in all the affairs of the world. Deep down in his nature there was a touch of Celtic mysticism. It sought expression in literary form, but his stories, though they were queer, were not of memorable quality. His "Life of Irving," however, is a noteworthy book. He had plenty of friends and enough enemies to indicate that his friendship was worth having. The embodiment of health and strength and geniality, it seems he died too young. He was only 64 years of age. Almost every one who knew him will say that he should have lived to be 90, and kept a young heart in his old age.

BIBLIOGRAPHY

"Adobe Days." *Robert Gavora, Fine and Rare Books.* Accessed November 12, 2011. http://www.robertgavora.com/shop/gavora/31377.html.

Barber, Paul. *Vampire, Burial, and Death: Folklore and Reality* (New Haven, CT: Yale University Press, 2010 [1988]).

Cain, Jr., Jimme E. *Bram Stoker and Russophobia: Evidence of the British Fear of Russia in Dracula and The Lady of the Shroud* (Jefferson, NC: McFarland, 2006).

Calmet, Augustin. *Dissertations sur les Apparitions des Anges, des Démons et des Esprits, et sur les Revenants et Vampires de Hongrie, de Bohême, de Moravie, et de Silésie* (Paris, 1746).

Cooper, Basil. *The Vampire in Legend and Fact* (Secaucus, NJ: The Citadel Press, 1974).

Farson, Daniel. *The Man Who Wrote Dracula: A Biography of Bram Stoker* (London: Michael Joseph, 1975).

Kaye, Marvin, ed., Introduction to *Dracula: The Definitive Edition* (Barnes & Noble Books, 1996).

Leatherdale, Clive, ed., *Dracula Unearthed* (Westcliff-on-Sea, UK: Desert Island Books, 1988).

Ludlam, Harry. *A Biography of Dracula: The Life Story of Bram Stoker* (London: W. Foulsham & Co., 1962).

Masters, Anthony. *The Natural History of the Vampire* (New York: G.P Putnam's Sons, 1972).

Eighteen-Bisang, Robert, and Elizabeth Miller. *Bram Stoker's Notes for Dracula: A Facsimile Edition* (Jefferson, NC: McFarland, 2008).

Eighteen-Bisang, Robert, and J. Gordon Melton. "*Dracula* in Print: A Checklist." In *Dracula in Visual Media: Film, Television, Comic Book and Electronic Game Appearances*. By John Edgar Browning and Caroline Joan (Kay) Picart (Jefferson, NC: McFarland, 2012): 265-272.

Halberstam, Judith. *Skin Shows: Gothic Horror and the Technology of Monsters* (Durham, NC: Duke University Press, 1995).

Kamîr, Ôrît. *Every Breath You Take: Stalking Narratives and the Law* (Ann Arbor, MI: University of Michigan Press, 2001).

Malchow, Howard L. *Gothic Images of Race in Nineteenth-Century Britain* (Palo Alto, CA: Stanford University Press, 1996).

Miller, Elizabeth, ed. *Bram Stoker's Dracula: A Documentary Journey into Vampire Country and the Dracula Phenomenon* (New York: Pegasus Books, 2009).

Moore, Leah, and John Reppion. Introduction to *Contemporary Review of "Dracula"* (Dublin: The Swan River Press, 2011).

McNally, Raymond T., and Radu Florescu. *In Search of Dracula: A True History of Dracula and Vampire Legends* (Greenwich, CT: New York Graphic Society Ltd., 1972).

"The Mysterious Stranger: A Tale." In *Chambers's Repository of Instructive and Amusing Facts* 8. No. 62 (London and Edinburgh: William and Robert Chambers, 1854): 1-32.

Pirie, David. *The Vampire Cinema* (New York: Crescent Books, 1977).

Riley, Philip J. *Dracula: The Original 1931 Shooting Script* (Atlantic City and Hollywood: MagicImage Film Books, 1990).

Stoker, Bram. *Dracula: A Mystery Story* (New York: W. R. Caldwell & Co., c.1918 [1897]).

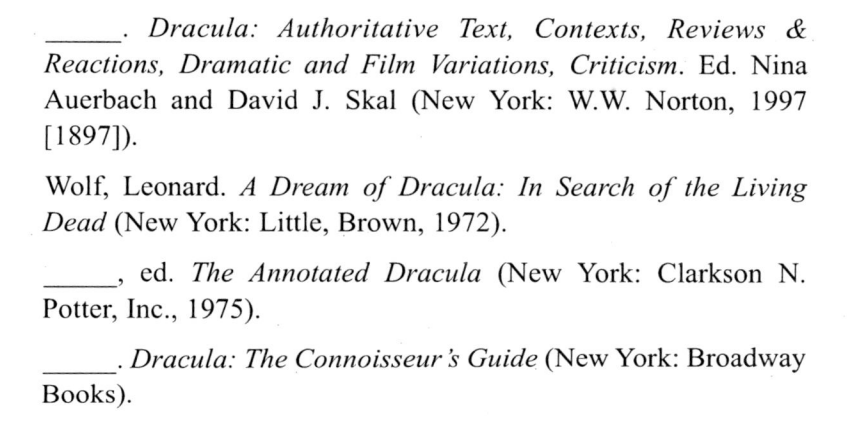

_____. *Dracula: Authoritative Text, Contexts, Reviews & Reactions, Dramatic and Film Variations, Criticism.* Ed. Nina Auerbach and David J. Skal (New York: W.W. Norton, 1997 [1897]).

Wolf, Leonard. *A Dream of Dracula: In Search of the Living Dead* (New York: Little, Brown, 1972).

_____, ed. *The Annotated Dracula* (New York: Clarkson N. Potter, Inc., 1975).

_____. *Dracula: The Connoisseur's Guide* (New York: Broadway Books).